TO THE GUTTER AND BACK

A Hull man's story

LEONARD BROMBY

Highgate Publications (Beverley) Ltd
1990

Home

Home is a place where I live,
Home is where I sleep,
Home is where I eat and drink,
Home is where I keep
All my memories, joyous and sad,
Memories of when I was just a lad.
Here comes the bulldozers covered in muck.
Spare my home? — No such luck!
To a new house I hold a key
But all that rubble is HOME to me.

All events described in this book are true, but some names have been changed to protect personal privacy.

British Library Cataloguing in Publication Data

Bromby, Leonard
    To the gutter and back: a Hull man's story.
    1. Alcoholism — Biographies
    I. 362.292092

ISBN 0-948929-36-7

Published by Highgate Publications (Beverley) Ltd.
24 Wylies Road, Beverley, HU17 7AP
Telephone (0482) 866826

Printed and Typeset in 10 on 11pt Plantin by
B.A. Press, 2-4 Newbegin, Lairgate, Beverley, HU17 8EG
Telephone (0482) 882232

ISBN 0 948929 36 7

Chapter One

EARLY MEMORIES

I have been told by the medical profession that my short-term memory is appalling, that my condition is the result of alcohol abuse, and is referred to as 'Alcoholic Amnesia'. My long-term memory seems to be unaffected, which is just as well, for my story begins with events which took place during the year 1940.

I was three years of age and World War Two was already spreading death around the globe. I had been born just one year and six days after the birth of my older brother Michael who entered the world on April 5, 1936. I arrived on April 11, 1937. We had a younger brother who had been born in 1939 . . . and mother was pregnant again! My immediate younger brother is called Jimmy. Mother was to be evacuated with us children, and our first destination after leaving our home in Hull was Bridlington.

It is Bridlington which gives me my first memory of childhood. I was leaning from a downstairs window as my mother approached the large house in which we were staying. Mother was carrying a small bundle in her arms. Ambulances were on reserve for more important things than a mother returning home with a new-born child. Michael and Jimmy were also looking from the window and a lady was saying to us young lads, 'Your mother is bringing you a new brother.'

The new arrival was to be called Dennis. Post-war was to bring four more brothers: Dennis then, *was* my youngest brother.

Our small family unit was split when we moved. Michael and myself were to stay with a family named Charnock who lived in Elizabeth Street, Halifax. Mother and the two younger lads were to stay with a very nice couple named Williams who lived in nearby Elland. Their home was called 'Omega' and it stood in Brian Road. Our father was due to be shipped out to the (forgotten) war in the Far East. Although there is a family photograph which shows Father with Mother and us four young boys, I have no memories of having seen him before the end of WWII . . . Perhaps it is just as well that I do not, for memories of that man are not happy memories.

I can just recall a few memories of the Charnock family and their home. Mrs Charnock was a small rounded woman who wore dark clothing. There was a lad named Arnold who kept rabbits (or mice) in a cage at the rear of a small yard, and another older brother who worked at a brick-making firm. I remember taking some sandwiches to the brick-works after the son had forgotten his 'packing up'. There was a large static water tank near to Elizabeth Street: I cannot recall what Mr Charnock did for a living, but whatever he did seemed to affect his feet! I can still picture the cast-iron fireplace which was familiar to most homes. A large tank at one side of the fire was for heating water, and the other side had an oven fitted. Mr Charnock sat at the side of the fire which housed the oven and I remember that he would remove his boots and his socks, roll a sock into a rope-like 'cleaner' and vigorously scrub between his toes. The rubbing was so vigorous that I wonder now how he did not burn his toes with friction.

Michael and myself were not to be separated from Mother and the two younger lads for long. Mother was given the tenancy of a corner shop which had been converted into a dwelling house. It was the year 1941 and mother was already homesick. Our new home was in Greetland, and I have a much clearer mental picture of that place. Our home stood at the top of a hill, and also at the corner of a small road. The postal address was Road End. There were many fields opposite our home, and it was from those fields that hares and rabbits made their dashes across the main road. Hedgehogs that had tried to emulate the quicker animals lay squashed, and flies and maggots had their fill. I remember the fields for their many colours . . . yellow buttercups, daisies, bluebells and maize, and a few bright red poppies.

There was a large public park at the bottom of the steep hill on which our home stood, and it was in that park that Michael lifted a rotten log which had been covering a nest of ants. The angry ants swarmed over my shoes and on to my legs. I cried with fright as brave Michael swept them away with his hands. I cannot remember whether I was stung or not. I do remember that there was a lot of stamping and crying as I sought to rid myself of the insects.

It was during the time we were at Greetland that I contracted the diseases of diphtheria and measles. I have a mental picture of my mother stroking my brow as she awaited the arrival of the ambulance which was to take me to the children's hospital. I have no memory of my stay at the hospital, but I do remember the day that I was released. I was sitting in a large room which had some toys on the floor, and there was a small girl who was also awaiting her parents. I do recall the short journey back to our temporary home. Mother wrapped blankets around me as I lay on a settee near to the warm fire. The only memory that I have of my illness is that I had a very sore throat.

My return home preceded some disturbing events which prompted Mother to return to Hull. The first thing to upset Mother was the hostility of the Greetland locals. Those clog-wearing folk referred to us as 'them thar furriners'. How strange, or perhaps primitive, was their attitude. We only came from a different part of the *same* county. I do not know if those locals ever had much to say to an old lady who lived in a basement flat, for her name was Miss Kendall and she was a Jewess from Germany. There was one very beautiful woman who befriended Mother, a lady named Elsie. There is a photograph in our family album which shows Elsie at her most charming, a lovely smiling woman. How sad that Elsie had the then fatal tuberculosis and was dying.

Mother was sometimes kept company by one of her sisters who travelled from Hull to stay with us for a while. Aunt Irene was younger than Mother, and Aunt Marjory was the youngest of all our aunts. Irene would dress herself up as the 'red-eyes' who took away noisy children. Lipstick around her eyes made her look the part. Marjory was more quiet-natured and Michael would tease her until she cried. Mother was very pleased to have company on one particular night, for a convicted rapist came knocking at her door. The seeds of fear and discontent had been sown. My adventurous brother Michael was almost to lose his life at Greetland. He climbed on to a glass roof that covered a factory which produced spun flax. The roof gave way under the weight of the adventurer and he plunged into the mill, narrowly missing the large upright spikes that held the bobbins. Michael was to have many accidents and many broken bones during his younger days.

Although there are no events which can be called really memorable, I shall always remember Greetland with affection, for those fields which were a blaze of yellow and green are so peaceful a memory compared to those which followed the return to Hull of Mother and us young lads. The year in which Mother had finally had quite enough of the clannish inhabitants of Greetland was 1941 — the time of the Blitz. I was almost five years of age and ready to begin school. I was also old enough to have the effects of war stamped indelibly into my mind. The peaceful scenes of Greetland were far different from the sight of wrecked homes. The peaceful nights were now ended as we slept in between the bombing raids. The wailing of the air-raid sirens which heralded death from the skies, the boom-boom of exploding bombs, and the dull thud of the anti-aircraft guns as they sought to blast the raiders from the skies . . . memories of families huddling together in the shelters, and memories of huddling beneath a staircase. Sad memories.

Families took to staying in their homes beneath the stairs, for a whole shelter-full were killed by a nearby blast. I can recall hearing the adults speak about the tragedy which took place in the Hessle/Anlaby Road area of Hull. The people in that shelter were said to have looked 'as though they were all asleep'. The general attitude after that tragedy was, 'Bugger the shelters.' I remember that the older folk would take a death-defying attitude as they lay in their beds during a raid: 'If it's got yer number on it, there's nowt yer can do about it!' They don't make people like that any more.

I remember seeing what we called 'darkies' in the city. The coloured American servicemen who — along with their white comrades — were said to be 'over paid, over sexed, and over here'. I had already learned the phrase, 'Have you got any gum, chum?' and remember those long flats of chewing gum which were given to cheeky young lads. I was wary of the black Americans, for young children who were naughty were often told, 'There is a black man waiting to get you!'

We returned to Hull when our Aunt Hilda (father's sister) was leaving her home in Vane Street. Mother was to apply for the tenancy of that home and be accepted, but not before we had spent a short time at the home of Grandmother. Those remaining few weeks with Grandmother were to be very hectic ones. We were living very close to Paragon Station which was a prime target for the German bomber. Some of those bombs were dropped very close to our home and many windows were shattered. A nearby church, St. Stephen's, received a direct hit (God was not guarding his property very well!) and our home shook with the blast. Just a hundred yards from the church there was a vicarage: it too received a hit . . . two to the devil that night! I remember women making comments such as, 'That was close,' and 'I hope the bastards haven't dropped one on my place; I've just white-washed the kitchen!'

There would sometimes be a few songs being sung, 'Hitler has only got one ball, Goering has got no balls at all,' and such favourites as, 'We're gonna hang out our washing on the Siegfried line.' Young lads would snigger as they joined in the bawdy singing and a mother would say, 'Hey, this is a grown-ups song.' A shaking of the shelter as a 'near thing' exploded had mothers wrapping protective arms around children. Women without children of their own would just grab the nearest child as the shelter shook. Some old man would say, 'We should have finished the bastards off last time.' A small boy asked, 'Why do the Germans want to kill us?' He was told, 'They are wicked, son, that's why,' and the boy asked, 'Will my dad get some bullets and kill the Germans?' 'Yes, love,' was the reply.

The day after a raid the damage was assessed. Broken windows were temporarily replaced with cardboard. There was no hope of repairing St. Stephen's church, and that building remained an eyesore for many years after the war had ended. It was also an adventure playground. One young lad lost his life when trying to obtain some of the eggs which had been laid by the pigeons that nested in the roof. He fell from the roof, landing on his head. Only yards from the old church another young person met a tragic death. The tailboard of a lorry fell and crushed the skull of a young girl. Both those deaths were all the more tragic for having occurred after the war had ended. Accidents had done what five years of enemy bombing had failed to do.

Easter 1942 brought me to my fifth birthday. I was ready for schooling. I remember how Aunt Marjory was still attending school, and it was she who took me to the Thomas Stratten School in Londesborough Street. I remember my first day at the school. A lady teacher was showing the class how to plait with raffia grass. I practised on mother's hair when I got home.

I was not to stay at the school for very long. Mother was told that the nearby Wawne Street School would have to take Michael and myself as pupils, for after we had moved into Vane Street we had shifted area. So I became a 'Wawne Street cat'. The Thomas Stratten pupils were known as 'Tommy 'Atten bulldogs'. The two schools often sent 'troops' against each other, and I remember singing the words, 'Tommy 'Atten Bulldogs, Wawne Street cats, when yer see a Wawny will yer please raise yer 'ats.' There were many street fights between the two schools — cobbles from the road were our main source of ammunition.

Schooling was not as efficient as teachers and parents would have liked it to be, for the nocturnal visits by enemy planes interrupted the sleep of both pupils and teachers. There could not be any sarcasm from a teacher asking, 'Have you been up all night?' for the answer would be a definite, 'Yes, sir,' and a tired young lad would stifle yet another yawn. Children who had been unable to get much sleep often fell into a snoring heap across their exercise books, and a teacher would ask for someone to 'give him a shove'. The sudden interruption of a loud snore would have us kids laughing helplessely. (I cannot help but chuckle as I write.)

There were many early morning raids by the bombers, and after having spent some time waiting for the all-clear we would always have a nice cup of tea. It really was impossible to sleep after a raid. I believe that the number of civilian deaths in Hull was more than 1,200. Many more were maimed. Thousands were mentally scarred for life.

Our schools were equipped with air-raid shelters, but I don't have any memories of daytime raids. Those shelters were used for kissing and cuddling sessions by the older boys and girls. Young children played doctors and nurses in the shelters, and adults used them at night for clandestine affairs. I reckon that quite a few of today's grand-parents were conceived in a concrete shelter. Wounded soldiers was another game that had me entering the shelters for 'treatment' . . . naughty, but nice!

In 1945 there was dancing in the streets. Buzzers were sounding the all-clear. Men and women were hugging and kissing in the streets, and there were tears of happy relief flowing down the cheeks of dancing people: those tears of relief were mingled with tears of sadness for those who had died during the conflict with Nazi Germany. It was all over. Bells rang out to herald the peace in Europe. People who were of a religious nature flocked to the churches to give thanks, and to say a special prayer for those citizens who had been the victims of the Blitz.

The end of the war in the Far East was to herald a new conflict for Mother and us four young lads. We were soon to suffer much cruelty, but not before we had first sampled the delights of our new home in Vane Street. We were not too distant from the home of our grandmother with whom we had spent those turbulent war years, and we were also close to the home of Father's mother and sister. The tradition of close-knit families was being upheld.

I remember very clearly how I ran up the stairs to explore our new home. My brothers and myself were claiming the room in which we wished to sleep. There were two bedrooms and a bathroom, plus two small attics. There was no water supply to the bath which acted as a makeshift bed until mother was given help by the Mother Humber Fund. We had to rely on charity for lots of things during those days of extreme poverty and hardship.

The restrictions which had been imposed upon us were now lifted. We could not slide down Grandma's bannister when we lived with her during the war, but we *could* slide down our own bannister. Games of hide-and-seek were great fun for us lads, and there were many places to hide. Cupboards upstairs and cupboards downstairs made good hiding places. We soon discovered that our home was just as infested as most homes were. Mice and rats, cockroaches, fleas and bugs. All were lodgers in our house . . . people who scratched themselves on the body or head would be asked, 'Have you got lodgers?' Cockroaches had a habit of crawling into clothing and shoes during the night, and so all clothing had to be thoroughly shaken each morning so as to dislodge them. I still recall with creeping flesh how I felt a tickle on my leg as I prepared for school. I looked down and saw a great red cockroach on my bare calf!

If one came downstairs during the night or the dark mornings of winter there would be hundreds of cockroaches covering the floors, and hundreds more could be seen covering the whole of the chimney-breast and the hearth. I had to make my way through the seething mass when I was given the task of making tea on a Saturday and Sunday morning. I would often protest against being chosen as tea-boy. 'But you always make the best cup,' said Mother. I was taken in by the patter, and so crunched my way through the black seething mass of creepie-crawlies as I made my way to the rat-infested scullery and the water tap.

I do not know who coined the phrase, 'the good old days', when referring to the Forties . . . careful thought prompts me to say, 'Good old days, my foot!'

Chapter Two

ENTER THE BEAST

The return of our father to the family home after the end of the war against Japan was the beginning of what was to be a period of regimentation, sadism, cruelty and violence. I cannot find words enough to describe those turbulent years of my childhood. The first thing that our father did was to give numbers to us lads. We were numbered by order of birth. It was very rare indeed that we would be referred to by name, and when father did use our name it would always be preceded by, 'That bastard.'

The drunkard who had taken over our home and shattered our happiness insisted upon being called 'The master'. Our arms would be twisted, or the short hairs on the back of our neck would be painfully twisted as we were asked, 'Who is the master?' and as we screamed out with pain we would manage to say the words, 'You are! you are!' I said those words more than once in a single day as the sadistic little ex-Lance Corporal demanded recognition of his command. Mornings were a painful experience during 'Inspection'. I would wince on having my ear pulled upwards, and stand on my tip-toes as I attempted to relieve the excruciating pain. A hard smack would precede the words, 'Get back to the sink and wash yourself again!' Washing for four young lads meant the sharing of just one bowl of water, for the master decreed that gas should not be wasted on the boiling of water for 'these f------animals.' I very soon realised that I hated this vain and grandiloquent little tyrant who tormented me. I longed for the war to start all over again so that he would have to go away again and leave us alone.

Mother dared not make too loud a protest at the treatment which was meted out, for previously having done so had resulted in the master smashing his fist into her mouth, saying, 'I'm in charge of this f-------house!' No-one was allowed to question the actions of the drunken animal who ate the rations of his children or sold them for drink. I hated those people who bought our rations and our clothing coupons. I hated them as they gave me a sweet, and a sickly smile as they said, 'Take this envelope straight home to your father.' I knew what was in the envelope. Cash for the master! Cash to be spent in a pretence of affluence as the master bought drinks for his friends.

Mother and us young lads were completely dominated by Father, so much so that we even had to request (army style) his permission before we spoke. A request to be allowed out to play had to begin with, 'Permission to speak, master?' Fingers were crossed as hopefully we lads awaited the answer. There were two answers which might be given: 'Yes, but only for one hour,' or the very depressing, 'No, you bloody-well can't, and get up those stairs now!' I well remember the attempt to escape being sent to bed. We asked mother if she would ask the beast for permission for us to play out. 'Definitely not,' said the master, and then, 'Get the bastards out of my sight. Send them to bed!' Oh well, we tried.

Father would sometimes say that my brothers and I could play outside if Mother would accept full responsibility for any bother we might get into. The order to go to our beds early in the evenings would have us wishing that we had not asked to be allowed to act like other children — children who played games. How well I remember those whispered conversations which we would hold as we sat on our beds in an unheated attic. 'When we grow up we can give him a good bashing-up.' We fantasized as to what we would do to the beast . . . 'We can pull his teeth out just like he does to us.' Father seemed to take great delight in pulling our teeth from their sockets, and would coax us into allowing him to pull a slightly loose tooth by offering money: 'I'll give you threepence if it hurts.' It always did hurt, but the master accused us lads of faking pain and gave us just one penny. Apart from expressing our desire to extract the teeth of the master, we also expressed the desire to beat him with the cable.

'The cable' was the most brutal weapon which the brutal ex-Lance Corporal was ever to use on our young and tender bodies. Father had often expressed his desire to find 'the ultimate method of punishment — one which will make these bastards obey my every command,' and, 'I want something which will ensure that they never step out of line again.' He found his ultimate weapon. Memories of the excruciating pain is felt forty years later as I write these words.

Father was doing some odd jobs about the home. Our landlord had commissioned the installation of electricity and the workmen had finished their task. A piece of thick cable was left behind by the workmen . . . 'Got it!' exclaimed our father as we marvelled at the electric lights, and failed to notice what 'it' was. We are soon to find out why he was so excited. 'This is the short end of cable,' he said, and then, 'I'll call it the short-end.' We were informed that the first one to step out of line would be able to experience being beaten with the cable and so be able to say whether it hurt or not. I do not remember which of us unfortunate lads was the first to be beaten with the cable, for we all received so many beatings so often. I do remember the first time that the terrible punishment was meted out to me. I screamed with the agony that the thick rubber sent through my body . . . the sheer pain as large blue bruises rose instantly on violated flesh. My scream for mercy fell upon deaf ears as the sadist wielded his ultimate weapon with rapid forehand and back-hand movements. I remember that I imagined that he was going to beat me to death. I made an attempt to wriggle under the draw-leaf table. My attempts to escape only served to encourage the master to attack in a more ferocious manner . . . he was most definitely *enjoying* the experience. I escaped further punishment by being sent to my bed. The master laughed with obvious delight, saying, 'I'll bet the bastard does as he is told in the future!' My vow to kill him when I grew large was renewed with even more hatred than before. I had never heard of the Marquis De Sade. I experienced the perverted lust of one who would do him credit. That evil little man who had so brutally beaten me with the cable must have been well satisfied, for my skin was broken and there was blood. I was unable to obtain sleep during the night after my first beating, for my wounds were painful and sore, and the huge and ugly bruises throbbed with pain. I had to stifle my sobs into my pillow lest the master issued a second beating because I was not acting 'like a man'.

Victorian attitudes were still very prevalent, and divorce was something that only the very rich could seek. There was no recourse for battered wives, for the unwritten law was, 'You've made your bed, now lie upon it!' Mother could not escape from Father by means of divorce, but even if she could have done so she would not have been able to keep us lads. There were no easy hand-outs in those days for women who left their husbands. Marriages were for life for the poor. Even the most determined woman would have to wait for seven years before obtaining a decree absolute *after* she had paid for her solicitor. We were lumbered with the beast.

Some of my school chums had fathers who were very much older than my own father, and those older men wore corduroy trousers which were held by large leather belts with large brass buckles attached. The old leather belts were used for meting out punishment, and offered two degrees of severity. A folded belt was used on a young lad who committed a minor offence. A more serious offence would merit being hit with the buckled end of the belt. 'A bloody good buckle-ending' would leave cuts and bruises. Of course, Father had a large buckled belt.

Another form of punishment would be to have the skin of our arms twisted in opposite directions — 'the Chinese burn', as such punishment was called. The general attitude towards women was that they should do as they were bade by their man of the house at all times. Women were expected to have a meal ready on time to coincide with the return home of the master of the house: he must never be kept waiting! A woman was expected to scrub a shirt until it was spotlessly clean, and she would have to starch the collars and cuffs and fold the shirt neatly. I well remember how Mother had to polish the shoes of our father if he stated that he would be going out in the evening (to spend our food money on drink and women) and there is little difference between memories of a Charles Dickens' novel, and the memories of our home . . . poverty and dominance and cruelty and violence.

The area in which our home was situated was centred around the rail and bus stations. Central Hull was very much like any other part of Hull when a family had a dispute. While families busied themselves in their separate households some event might take place which would result in a gathering of hordes of relatives. 'Hit one of us and you hit the bloody lot!' resulted in many memorable street battles. Uncles and aunts, brothers and sisters, cousins and in-laws — families really did stick together. If a person came home after having taken a beating which was deemed to have been unfair, unjustified, or just unacceptable because it had been given by an outsider (someone from a different district), then the whole family would gather together and march upon the home of the offending party. Orders were given to young lads to, 'Go and get yer Uncle Fred, and tell 'im ter bring the lads.' The lads referred to were the sons of Fred. I remember how very exciting an occasion it was as whole families marched through the streets towards the scene of battle. 'There's gonna be ding-dong!' cried some young lad, and hordes of excited young children would follow the avenging army of kinfolk as they marched upon the enemy. Even friends would join the affray if they happened across the marchers. 'What's up, then?' asked a friend. 'Wiv gorra bitta bother on,' would be the reply. 'Ahm cummin wi yer then,' said the friend as he spat upon his hands and then rubbed them together. Eager young spectators would be told to, 'Gerrout the way!' by their elders as shirt sleeves were rolled up and large leather belts were removed from the waist ready for use as weapons, buckled ends swirling.

As the avenging family reached their destination there would be a cry of, 'Come on out, you bastards, let's be having you!' and there would be a loud banging on a front door. Persistent banging would bring someone to the door to declare, 'Yer all mouth now, yer bastards, but wait 'til our lot get 'ere!' There would be accusations of cowardice and of men hiding beneath stairs, afraid to come out of doors. Some man or woman would emerge from the besieged house and state, 'You'll regret the day that you started shouting around here.' Suddenly a cry of, 'They're here!' would be heard. The family of the besieged were approaching the scene. As the two armies met in the street there would be a shout of, 'Right, then. Which of you bastards wants it fost?' Women who had a child in one arm would have a broom in the other hand, and it was not at all unusual to see those women join in the affray.

Young lads kicked the shins of the enemy, or pulled at the hair of a man who had the upper hand of one of their family. Women screamed as they fought on the floor, and excited young lads pointed as they saw all that the woman had beneath her skirts — knickers were expensive items, and so were not always worn by the economy-minded women. Mops and sweeping brushes were always a part of the armoury, and, although the occasional poker would be brandished, I cannot recall ever seeing one being used on the head of an opponent. The street fight would never last for any length of time, and it was usually ended with a cry of, 'Oh, bloody hell! Look at his head!' A badly gashed head and the sight of blood was enough to end the affray. Before the battle ended there would be plenty of screaming and shouting as women tore handsful of hair from enemy scalps. The fights ended as some spokesman shouted, 'That's enough!' and both sides began to draw back from each other. Once the fighting had come to an end some person would say, 'Let that be a lesson to you not to mess with our lot.' After a bit of shouting and a few accusations of dirty fighting there would be handshakes all round. There were occasions when some refused to shake hands as they said, 'You haven't heard the last of this,' but it was very rare for a fight to resume later, if at all.

The day after a street battle usually saw young lads taunting each other with remarks such as, 'Our Fred clouted your Ernie in the gob and he backed away too scared to fight!' Arguments began as lads taunted each other with allegations of cowardice, and so playground fights took place until a teacher broke up the affray. Lads usually formed a circle around the two antagonists and chanted, 'Eee-Ooo! Eee-Ooo!' as they urged the fighters on. Many solid and long-lasting friendships were formed by lads who had fought against each other.

Most of the housing during my younger days was without an indoor toilet. Night-time visits were a very scary affair as I dashed to our outside toilet. I never have liked the darkness, and venturing into a dark yard at night was very frightening. I would sit forward with my hand holding the door: my heart would pound as I imagined some stranger to be lurking in the darkness. Mother would stand at the back door of the house until I got seated. 'Are you on?' 'Yes.' 'Well, shout when you are ready to come off,' said Mother. I would imagine all sorts of things as I sat in the darkness trying to rush to job. 'Mam, I'm finished!' I shouted in a blind panic as my imagination ran wild. Although it was only a distance of a few feet between the house and the toilet I shivered with fear as I dashed back to the sanctuary of the indoors.

If Father was in the house when a nocturnal visit to the toilet was needed, I had to cross my fingers that I would be allowed to make the visit at all! My brothers and myself were usually told to, 'Bake it until the morning,' by that nasty little man who did not wish to be disturbed. Mother had to plead with him to allow us lads to visit the toilet. Lots of arguments were caused by his refusal to allow this. 'If the bastards went to bed and slept, they would not need to go before the morning!' was one of his stupid and selfish arguments. I remember being given the task of emptying the buckets which my father kept in *his* bedroom. It was a very slow journey down the stairs as I sought to stop the overful bucket from spilling its contents of acrid urine.

Small terraces were numerous down each side of very long streets. Those terraces contained small houses which never saw the light of the sun shining through a window. Nice names like Villa did not alter the fact that the houses were in a terrace. The only difference was that a villa provided a very small amount of earth at the front of the house. Young girls who bounced their rubber ball against a wall did not realise that the very thin walls allowed many annoying 'Bump, bump, bump' to sound inside the house. Irate inhabitants would emerge to say, 'Go and bounce your ball elsewhere.' Many families had heated arguments over their children.

'Dark Satanic mills' was an apt description of northern towns, and there was no shortage of such buildings in Hull. One such building was what was called Cocoa Mills. There was a very fierce fire which enveloped the mills, trapping a man by his leg as falling timbers endangered life and limb. The then police surgeon, Dr. P. M. Scott, amputated the leg of the unfortunate worker. The amputation was carried out with the help of a pocket-knife and courage by both men. The building was in danger of collapsing. There was a large complex which stood at the main road end of the street in which our family were living after the end of WWII, known as Blundell's building at one end, and Blundell's Corner at the other end, and the centre of the complex was called Pointer's after the doll-making and toy wholesale firm which was situated there. Scrapped arms and legs of plastic material, along with heads and bodies, formed a large rubbish tip from which young girls would take the parts and make a doll — there were some dolls which would have done credit to Frankenstein! Young lads were able to find imperfect toy soldiers. The large buildings were demolished during the 1980s.

It is strange how those buildings which had been my playground as a lad were to become my shelter as I tramped the streets of Hull during my years as a vagrant. I was to wander through the large and deserted complex looking for somewhere to shelter from the elements and the society that scorned me for my predicament. Childhood days are remembered with some nostalgia. Happier moments of a childhood which was filled with violence return as I remember the ice-cream carts which were searched by young lads. Small and grubby hands were thrust into the very small space between cart and ice-cream tub. 'I've found a penny!' shouted one boy, and there would be an immediate cry of, 'Arf yags av ad yer!' which meant, 'Half shares, I claimed from you!'

The grubby faces of young lads from long ago are still fresh within my memory as I recall the Hull of yesteryear, my Hull. I find it difficult to adapt to the sight of modern houses that are, in the words of the song, 'all made out of ticky-tacky and they all look just the same — little boxes'. The small terraces of yesteryear would be filled with wooden chairs as the occupants of sun-starved and gloomy homes emerged to bathe in the sunlight. Because gas-lit homes were not very brightly lit, people would shield their eyes from the sudden brightness of daylight which greeted them as they emerged from their damp and gloomy abodes. Large tin baths would be brought into the terraces, and, after many trips in and out of the home to fill pans with water, the baths would be used as paddling pools for very small children. Bathing costumes which had been obtained from jumble sales would be worn by the happy children who found the tin baths a wonderful substitute for the seaside which they had never seen. Such scenes are among my most pleasant memories: a wooden spoon being used to make splashes as some rosy-cheeked little infant sat in an old tin bath, a picture of innocence, totally unaware of the better things in life, children who had never even seen such a luxury as a banana. If a child had a small rubber duck to float in the water, then that duck had most definitely been a charitable gift from some rich home where a child had tired of it. As the small children played, old men with wizened faces would sit twisting old rope into lanyards. Fancy knots would be tied and untied as the men whiled away the time. Some men would indulge in feats of strength as they sat a small child on a wooden chair, and then lifted the chair with one hand. I found it difficult to lift the chair more than a few inches from the ground. The men lifted the child and the chair by holding just one of the chair's legs.

Old folk laughed along with the youngsters, showing black stumps which had once been teeth as their lips parted with laughter. I cannot recall any old person who had a full set of decent teeth to show. I remember how, after the war, lots of the older people obtained false teeth which they could not cope with. The teeth were large and uncomfortable and horsey. Old folk would have a handkerchief handy at meal times so that they could cover their mouth and remove the ill-fitting teeth. Most folk looked as though they were participants in a gurning contest as they chomped their food with hardened gums.

Tug-o-war games were very popular events in which both men and women took part. There were some very strong women when I was a young boy, for women in those days worked very hard. No fancy carpet cleaners for them, no washing machines or easy-to-use launderettes. Uncarpeted floors were scrubbed clean each day, as was the front doorstep and window sill. I remember how the older and more domineering type of women would stand with their huge arms folded, looking rather dominant and very authoritative. Women who were well built would often fight with men who annoyed them. There was no hair-pulling either — those huge women clenched their fists and confronted a man with the words, 'Come on, let's be 'avin yer!'

The wall of a cul-de-sac would be marked with white chalk to represent a wicket and, with the aid of a piece of wood and a rubber ball, a game of cricket would be played. There was always some person who would hit a ball far too hard and so break a window and spoil the game. Culprits were made to make good the damage even if it meant many weeks of saving their spare half-pennies. Cardboard filled the gap until a window was fitted.

Some of the balls that were hit too hard had very serious consequences attached to them as a young person ran to retrieve them. Before the War horses and carts were the main means of transport, so youngsters did not have anything to fear as they ran after a ball that had left the terrace. Post-war years saw the gradual introduction of delivery vans and lorries. There were many very serious accidents before people became accustomed to the fast moving motorised vehicles. There were some deaths too.

Memories of the old terraces would not be complete without a mental picture of the lines of freshly scrubbed washing which were hung out to dry each washday. Lines of clean washing would present a problem for any stranger who wished to visit one of the terraced homes. 'What do you want? What are you after?' would be the question asked of a stranger. Hostile eyes would focus on the intruder. 'Watch what you're doing, I've just spent hours scrubbing that lot.'

Memories of washday in our home are memories of a boiler in the shed, a large and very old wringer, and two washing lines stretched across a back yard. The boiler was a small cast-iron basin set in a brick structure which had space for a small fire to be lit. Clouds of smoke would billow from the shed before the fire began to 'draw' properly. Having finally managed to get the fire to go and the water heated to boiling, Mother would begin the task of scrubbing the family wash. A small wooden table was used for the clothing to be placed upon as it was scrubbed. A 'dolly' tub was used for the items which did not need to be scrubbed, and a 'dolly' stick to move the washing around in the tub. Mother would twist the dolly stick back and forth in the tub until it was considered that the clothes would be clean. The clothes were wrung first by hand, and then put through a wringer. If the old wringer broke down, then Mother had to wring extra hard by hand before pegging the washing to the lines. If a cog broke on a wringer a search of the scrap metal dealers would hopefully provide a replacement. Some cogs were welded on the sly by a friend who worked as a welder, but not many families knew of such workers and so wringers would be scrapped when they broke, and the money from the scrap would buy food.

Memories of washdays are memories of fresh smelling sheets flapping in the wind as they dried — that lovely clean smell fills my nostrils as I write, and I picture Mother brushing aside the hair from her eyes with the back of a wet hand, a heaved sigh, and she starts scrubbing again. 'Shall I scrub some for you, mam?' 'No, but you can put the kettle on and make me a nice cup of tea.' I did my bit by making 'the best cup of tea I've had'. Thanks, Ma!

Parents who had sons and daughters in a two-bedroomed house would use a blanket as a screen at bedtime, for it was necessary for boys and girls to share. The youngest child of a family usually slept with parents until he or she was considered old enough (maybe two years) to share a bed with an older brother or sister. A boy who became a bit too mature would sleep downstairs on a couch or two chairs that were pushed together — very uncomfortable. Lots of mature young lads either went to sea or joined the army — how else could they escape the overcrowding? If a small one-bedroomed house became available, then young people would marry and move in. There were many teenage marriages as boys and girls from crowded homes sought some freedom and privacy, and there were many tears of regret when young couples found out they were not really compatible, but they stayed with each other 'for the sake of the kids'. Lots of marriages were between childhood sweethearts, for families tended to stick to their own community area, and even jobs were passed from one family member to another as a man retired through age or injury. Many firms had a father and son and a grandfather working side by side. Strangers were people who came from any other area of Hull, even if that other part was just a few streets away. Burglars did not usually steal from the poor, but any who wished to do so would soon be deterred as a watchful neighbour challenged: 'You're not from around here — who are you looking for?

The Hessle Road area of Hull was made famous in a song. Most people associate Hull with the fishing industry and form the opinion that all our men go to sea, all our women mend trawl nets, and that we all live on fish. Most of the fish packaging is done in the Hessle Road area, for the fish-docks are situated in that area, as are the packaging industries. It is not just the Hessle Road people who are clannish. I feel as though I am in a diffferent town if I venture to other areas of Hull. There is not so much difference now between the different areas of my home town, for modern estates and high-rise flats have made all areas look the same, and, as the rehousing of people took place, the huge family clans were broken. Lots of families applied for exchanges so that they could be 'near to our own'. Such exchanges were not always readily available . . . the community spirit began to die.

'Lazy dockers' was a much-used expression when I was a young lad, and the old Princes cinema was called 'Dockers' Rest' by older folk who intimated that dockers slept in the seats of the cinema instead of working. The cinema is now used as a night club, and other cinemas have been converted into bingo halls. The National cinema in Beverley Road was converted into a bowling alley that later burned down, and all that remains of that place where I watched so many cowboy matinees on a Saturday afternoon is an area of concrete with weed-filled cracks. An adjoining building was used as a snooker hall, and it was in that snooker hall that I learned how to mis-spend my youth. My friend Ron and paid 2¾d per hour for the use of a table during the early 1950s.

I have heard older people say, 'Things ain't what they used to be,' and I agree. Much has been done that has destroyed those visual reminders of my boyhood. An ancient public house which was the subject of a long legal battle was eventually pulled down to make way for a car park — the leaning pub which was propped up with wooden supports, the Zoological. I spent many hours wishing a 'merry Xmas' to the patrons of the old pub when I was a lad, and I spent many hours drinking in it after I had turned 17. The trams that I rode on for just a halfpenny are long gone, and the trolley buses that replaced them are gone too. But the memory of those large blue vehicles is still with me. They often came to a sudden halt as the overhead supply rods became detached. There were huge hooked poles that fitted into long tubes beneath the old buses, and the conductor would withdraw one of the huge poles and re-connect the arms to the overhead supply.

The shells of what were once prosperous warehouses have been converted into homes for the rich and the prosperous. The idle rich use our once busy docks as marinas, and the large warehouses have been converted into luxury apartments that overlook the moored yachts which have replaced the barges that carried a cargo and working men.

The old warehouses provide many memories of a bygone age . . . Sweating men wearing cloth caps and collarless shirts with sleeves rolled up past the elbow to reveal faded blue tattoos which had been inscribed during the Great War. Those old men had skins like leather that had been well worn, supple and filled with deep furrows. A large platform which was attached to chains would be lowered from a doorway of one of the many floors of a warehouse. The platform (or pallet) would be loaded with sacks of grain, or other goods such as cartons of canned food. There were no hydraulic or electric lifting devices, and men would raise loaded pallets by pulling on chains and/or stout ropes — manpower was the order of the day as loads were winched upwards, and men would lean precariously as they stretched their arms forwards to grasp hold of a pallet and steer it into the doorways of the upper floors of the warehouse. Those sweating and grunting men are just a memory as some person pours another drink, and passes another plate of salmon sandwiches in a fancy docklands luxury apartment that had once held grain.

The sound of some man shouting, 'Whoa, yer bastard!' as a huge and impatient carthouse pounded the cobbled stones with a slow and steady movement. Sparks would shoot from the flintstone cobbles as the huge metal horseshoes made their sliding contact with the ground. The smell of huge beasts is still fresh within my nostrils. Huge, magnificent, strong . . . how can one find words enough to describe those beasts of burden? Clouds of steaming breath being exhaled from huge and gaping nostrils, a chomping of huge yellow teeth around the bit. I would put my hand forwards as I gingerly stroked the powerful, sweating animal. The horses were always quite warm to the touch.

I would quickly withdraw my hand from a sweating flank as the animal snorted and turned its huge head in my direction, and showed its teeth as it raised an upper lip and sprayed spittle with a 'Shhhh' and a 'Brrrr' combined into one sound. The workman who was unloading (or loading) a cart would say, 'Aye, lass, it'll not be long now,' and then a change of tone as the horse took a couple of steps forward, causing a sack or carton to be dropped. 'Whoa, yer bastard — givower!' Passing a stationary horse was always a time for caution, for a sudden turn of the huge head could knock a cyclist from his machine into the path of oncoming traffic. Pedestrians could receive a blow that would send them falling to the floor. The horses regularly turned their heads as a gesture of impatience. Smaller and more appealing horses were used to pull smaller carts such as those which were used by the rag-and-bone merchants. The smaller horses would often be startled by the sounds of motorised transport, and I have often witnessed the sight of some irate merchant standing with the reins in his hands as he attempted to halt a frightened runaway. Shouts of, 'Gerrout the way! Gerrout the way!' were the only means of giving warning to the public. The frightened animals were as unfamiliar with the motorised traffic as were those unfortunate children who were knocked down in the streets. To run home and attempt to relate the story of a runaway horse would bring scorn from my father as the excitement in my voice (or the voices of my brothers) would bring a sneer to the face of the beast: 'You silly little bastard, you sound like a tart!' We were not allowed to show anything other than a manly image.

Most of the men who worked as manual labourers were dressed in a like manner. Cloth caps, blue striped waistcoats, corduroy trousers which were held at the waist by a large leather belt, and hob-nailed boots. A coloured neckerchief around a collarless neck, and very short hair which was known as 'a short back and sides'. Aftershave was 'summat fer poofs' or 'bloody scent'. I tend to agree with the latter and feel awful when I use my Christmas aftershave or air-freshener pads. I do wish that my family and my female friends would stop telling me that I should 'Stop being old-fashioned.' I remember how old men with steely eyes that had witnessed trench warfare would look at those younger men with long hair and say, 'It's gerrin' 'ard ter tell which is men an' which is wimmin these days!' Those old men would find it even more difficult now that earrings and necklaces and bracelets adorn the bodies of registered males! Our regimented father would cut the hair of my brothers and myself so that it stood barely one eighth of an inch high from our scalp. He called such a style a 'punishment' cut, and issued such cuts instead of a beating. We were given a choice, 'Do you want some 'short end of cable' or shall I get the scissors out?' The scissors won over the terrible agony which a beating with the heavy-duty cable would inflict.

Memories of my schooldays are plentiful, and it is with the utmost pleasure that I recall those games which were played by schoolboys. Small informative cards were included in a packet of cigarettes and were known as 'ciggies'. The small cards portrayed wildlife, ships, aeroplanes or any subject of interest. The cigarette cards were used to play the game of 'ciggies' by means of one lad standing a card against a wall, and allowing other lads to flick cards in an attempt to knock down the standing card. All cards that failed to achieve their objective would be forfeit. Marbles were very popular and there were many variations of the game, the two most common being 'holey' and 'nearest'. The game of holey was played by aiming one's marble at a distant pole in the ground. The marble which was the nearer to the hole gave its owner the first go at the other marbles. The marble nearest to the hole had to be rolled into the hole before a shot at the opposition would be permitted. Nearest was played mostly as a street game, for there were no holes available in some streets. The marble which was nearest to the wall would give the privilege of the first choice of shot to its owner. If the first shot was close to the hole, then other players could just drop their marble on to the ground, well away from the hole. Only the bravest of boys would attempt to beat a very near shot, for a marble that landed just a couple of inches from the hole was most definitely a lost marble! It seems just a short while ago that a raggy-arsed young lad became involved in a game of marbles and completely forgot about a violent and sadistic father. I showed my young son how to play marbles during the 1960s and it was the most enjoyable day I have ever had.

Young lads who did not have a marble during the Forties tore strips of tar from the side of the road and made 'tarogs' by softening the tar in a warm hand. The tar would be rolled around in the palm of the hand until it formed a nice rounded shape, and then left to harden. Tarogs were not given any value. Plain glass marbles were swapped at the rate of two for one coloured glass marble, or three for a ball-bearing (bollie).

Trading or swapping was a common practice among young lads who had grown tired of their old toys. Pockets would bulge as young lads crammed old toys into them. Most of my toys had been charitable gifts from the Mother Humber Fund: Teachers would allow us to carry out our swaps and trades during playtime, and some teachers even gave us a few pence for articles that could be used by their own children.

Lead soldiers and catapults, comics and cap guns and old annuals, and pea-shooters. All were traded in the school playground. I well remember how I made my clothing appear to be more ragged and worn than it already was, and then opened the door of the Mother Humber Fund shop and asked for some toys: 'Missis, ayah gorrenny toys?' I was given a comic, and a jig-saw puzzle, and a cap-gun. I told mother that I had won those things when playing marbles. I said that I had won lots of marbles and then swapped them. One source of used comics was the dump of the Victoria Children's Hospital. I would rake through the hospital refuse for comics that I could first read and then barter for other goods. Home-made wooden guns, bows and arrows and catapults were quite popular. I only know of one case where the indiscriminate use of a bow resulted in a tragedy. A young lad lost the use of an eye.

Chapter Three

ALL THE FUN OF THE FAIR

Hull Fair is an event to which most people look forward each year. The fair was always a great attraction to me when I was younger. I spent many happy hours just wandering around the many stalls and side-shows. I gazed with not very much enthusiasm as some man extolled the virtues of Christianity, and I wondered why a God-botherer chose a fun-fair as a preaching ground. Perhaps he was one of the old Hellfire and brimstone brigade. I would watch out for those side-shows where scantily clad and shapely women beckoned custom: 'Roll up now, the show is about to begin — no waiting.' The Wild West shows provided the most beautiful girls for a young lad to fantasize over, and, as I stood looking up at those curvaceous young bodies and lovely long legs, I fantasized as only a growing young lad can.

The firing of blank cartridges and the cracking of whips, the 'Eeagh!' sound which the girls made, and the banging of a drum all had me fascinated. I never have seen a Wild West show, for I never had enough money to see one when I was young. Conscription denied me the chance to see shows when I would have been able to earn enough money. Later years were to be spent drinking in public houses, and, although I did visit Hull Fair, I found it noisy and commercialised. The attractions which I so much enjoyed at the fair have all been replaced by bingo stalls. I still have my memories of the steam organs and the shamrock, and the smell of hotdogs and candyfloss, and fish and chips. I remember how the sound of a steam organ would eventually draw me away from the Wild West show girls . . . one last look at long shapely legs which were so prominently displayed beneath the hemlines of short tasselled skirts . . . one last look at those short white briefs would be followed by a long sigh.

I would move away in the direction of the shamrock. I have never ridden on the shamrock, never seen a Wild West show or a boxing display, and I have never had my fortune told by any of the many experts who line the street in which the fairground is sited. I may decide to go to the fair one day and do lots of those things that I did not do as a lad — see the flea circus, watch the boxing, take a deep breath and enter the Wild West show tent. The dodgem cars were always a fascinating attraction as showers of sparks flew from overhead power arms, and nimble-footed attendants leapt from one moving car to another as they collected the fares. I would often wish that I was one of those rich college kids so that I could afford to ride on the cars, see the side shows, buy toffee apples and pomegranates, or fish and chips, cinder toffee and candy floss. I could only look longingly at the hot-dogs with onions, the roasted chestnuts and the coconuts.

Many young men were still wearing uniforms during the late 1940s as they awaited demobilisation after the recently ended war. I remember the laughing servicemen goading each other, 'Go on, have a go at him,' as they stood outside the boxing booth listening to the barker offering £5 to the man who could stay for three rounds with the champ. £5 was almost a week's wages for a working man in a low-paid occupation. I remember hearing adults speak of a wage of just £8 per week. I was only paid that amount in 1958. Wage claims in those far-off days were for as little as a half-a-crown which was equal to 12¾p. Married men asked for an increase of five shillings (25p).

During Hull Fair week I would try to earn as much as I could by running errands for neighbours, and like most young lads I wanted to visit the fair every day. Even without money I would visit the fair as often as I could. The many fortune tellers who offered their services at the fair would all claim to be the original descendant of some ancient Egyptian. Photographs of celebrities were on display, and the fortune teller would claim to be the only one that the celebrity would consult.

One stallholder who really caught my attention was a man who was selling bird warblers. I had always been fascinated by the talents of Ronnie Ronalde who imitated birds on the radio. I put my hand in my pocket and withdrew the 3¾d that I had left. The bird warblers were priced at 6d. 'I'll give yer threppence 'a'penny for one,' I offered. I tried to look poverty-stricken and dejected as I held out my hand. 'Piss off!' said the man. 'I'm not a bloody charity.' Despite the rudeness of the stallholder I stayed and listened to his melodious trilling for a while before making my way home. As I walked away I would turn my head and watch the big wheel as it turned around in the darkness. I could still hear the excited screams of young girls who rode on the wheel. The sounds of the steam organs began to grow faint and the big wheel became a distant glimmer as its many lights faded in the October mist. I rounded a corner into the street in which I lived, and the sights and the sounds were gone. It was a tired and sad young boy who climbed into his bed. 'I wish that I could have bought a bird warbler,' I mumbled before falling asleep.

Although there were many street parties which took place after the end of the war, I can only remember having attended one of those parties. I was embarrassed about the usual procedure of children having to take a contribution towards the party — flour, sugar, lard etc. Poor Mother was kept so short of money by my father that she could barely afford to buy a loaf for our home. 'You will have to go without sugar in your tea for a couple of days if I give you some to take to the party,' said Mother. My brothers and myself agreed to do without so that we could have a bit of dignity as we joined other children. There was never any discrimination against families who could not manage to make a contribution, but to a growing young lad who knew what poverty and charity were it could be very embarrassing to sit and eat with those children who were from 'better-off' families. Some spiteful little bastard of a kid from a more affluent family would sometimes pass the remark, 'I'll bet their mam didn't give anything.' I was far too shy and reserved to retaliate, and just sat in my seat aware that my face had turned bright red. I dislike rich people.

I felt guilty when accepting a paper hat to wear, I felt as though I should be touching my forelock. I felt guilty for accepting a small bottle of lemonade. I tried to politely refuse many things at the party but had them forced upon me by some pleasant lady who insisted, 'Come on now, no need to be shy.' I chewed the food very slowly, not daring to show that I was not used to such luxurious fare. I hated the fact that I was from a poor family and wished that Mother could meet a really nice rich man and run away from my dad.

My brothers and myself would often express such a wish. Mother would approach party organisers and request that we brothers be allowed to wash pots after the party was over — helping would alleviate the feeling of inferiority that charitable acts bestowed upon me. I form an immediate dislike of people who attempt to give me something (such as a cigarette) after I have said, 'No.' I am reminded of those days when I was urged, 'Go on, love, there are plenty to go round,' and I took a bun from a plate as my face went a bright red with embarrassment.

I never felt comfortable at public events, for children who were better-off were always dressed in their Sunday best whilst my brothers and myself were wearing the only clothes we had, which were our everyday, well-worn and well-patched second-hand clobber. Despite the fact that our clothing was worn and second-hand, Mother ensured that all our togs were clean and well ironed and well patched. Even the Dandy and the Beano comics would show kids with patches in their pants!

Attending a Sunday school caused as much embarrassment as attending a party because of poverty. Father had insisted that we attend a Sunday school so that we would be 'Out of the f------way, and out of my f------sight.' The Sunday school organised a trip to the sea-side and, because my brothers and I had no money, took myself and Jimmy and Dennis free of charge. Michael had his friends and I hardly knew him as we all grew older. He was a bit of a bully and took delight in being nasty when left in charge of us.

Michael would add salt to a cup of water if we complained of being thirsty, and he also took delight in some arm twisting. I cannot recall Michael ever joining my two younger brothers and myself in any games. He was more adventurous and so joined other lads who went camping and who enjoyed a swim in Barmston Drain. It was by choice that Michael estranged himself from us. I remember how he would tell me to get lost if I asked to go with him, and on one occasion he coaxed one of his friends into fighting me. I remembered my straight-left teaching and fought the other boy back to his own home, which was about fifty yards away from where the fight began.

It was many years ago that I went to the sea-side with the Sunday school which was near to our home, but the memory of my return home is still very clear. 'We went on the sand and a lady paid for a donkey ride for us!' I said excitedly. The animal who ruled our home grabbed hold of me roughly. 'You have been begging then have you, you f------bastard?' I was given a beating, as were Jimmy and Dennis, and we were sent to our beds. There is no doubt at all that the conscience of the master had been pricked as he saw the enjoyment that other people had bought for me. 'You'll go to bed straight after school for the next three days,' said the master, and then, 'I'll teach you not to show me up!' My hatred grew stronger as I lay in the dark attic. 'I'll be big enough to get him one day,' I told myself. One occasion when I got the better of my father was after I had been told to attend Sunday school but had gone to the park instead. I returned home at the time that the Sunday school would have finished. The master thought that he would catch me out if he asked me a question on what I had learned at Sunday school. 'We were taught about the loaves and fishes,' I replied. The master was then satisfied that I had attended. It was a very nice and very uplifting feeling when I was able to put one over on him. My brothers also indulged in the deception, and our mother was let into the secret so that we could all enjoy laughing behind his back.

Explorations into what was deemed to be the affluent area of Hull were made by my brothers and myself during the long summer holiday away from school. The Avenues area of Hull was a residential area which was known as the posh part of our city. The very rich business people began to move away from the Avenues as the bed-sitter landlords moved in. The large houses that had been so well kept, and the gardens that had been so well cultivated all went to ruin as money-grabbing and unscrupulous people began to buy the houses for conversion into flats. The outer woodwork began to deteriorate as old paint cracked and fell away.

My memories of the affluent areas cannot be erased by the bulldozers. I would ask Mother if I could borrow the pram that was usually used for taking my two younger brothers to the park. I used the pram as I went round the Avenues to collect old rags and jars. When my brothers accompanied me we would argue over rags. A lot of those so-called rags were far superior in condition to the clothes that we were wearing. How exciting it was to find a good pair of trousers that were not worn and patched, and a pair of shoes that were not down on the heel and worn through at the sole. Providing that a pair of shoes or a garment was not too large or too small — those items were considered to be a good fit. Some of the clothing was in such good condition that Mother was able to pawn it. Pawning some item would enable her to supplement the sparse amount of money which our selfish father gave for housekeeping. Other items of clothing would be the cause of much squabbling. 'I collected this shirt, it's mine,' said one of us lads. Mother would decide the issue of who had any particular item of clothing. Her word was final.

My Hull of yesteryear is gone. A bulldozer smashes down a row of homes that had withstood the might of the Luftwaffe. Another block of ticky-tacky boxes is erected and called a housing estate.

We who were taken from our homes now have all the luxuries — indoor toilets and hot water, central heating, and draught-free homes. We have *lost* the doorstep conversations. We have *lost* the conversations which were held over a garden wall or fence. We are unable to watch our neighbours' front and back doors if they go away for a day. We are unable to see the lurking strangers who may be intent on burglary. We do not get to know people any more as we did when the corner shop was filled with customers waiting to be served. We go through a supermarket serving ourselves, and a machine tots up the bill. No friendly conversations are held with a shop assistant. A girl on a checkout stares into space as we attempt to put our goods into a carrier bag. She starts emptying another basket as we are still trying to pick up the last few items of our paid for goods.

I live in a flat which is sited over one of the fields in which I gathered mushrooms during the late 1940s. Perhaps my flat is sited on the spot where I hacked away at a tree for a piece of wood that was suitable for the making of a catapult? Playthings for young lads who had been brought up in an atmosphere of war and destruction consisted of replica weapons. Catapults were a regular feature of a young lad's arsenal and, because there were plenty of bomb-wrecked buildings, there was a constant supply of ammunition. I shudder when I recall some of those games in which I took part as a lad. Along with many other lads of my own age I would set up a target of an old tin and practise with my catapult. It was never too long before some lad suggested that sides should be taken for a 'catty-fight'.

It would seem that there was an irresponsible attitude shown by young lads who fought amid the rubble of a world war, but we did not go mugging old ladies as some youngsters do today. We youngsters ran errands for the elderly and also washed their windows and dug their gardens. We respected our elders. Money would be given by old folk who could afford to reward lads for doing odd jobs, but we did not mind doing the jobs for free when we knew that some old lady was poor. One dear old lady provided myself and my two younger brothers with a cup of cocoa each as we cleaned her front path of snow and ice, and her action prompted us to call the lady 'Cocoa'. The name stuck, and it was during the early 1950s when, as a teenager, I was given the sad news that 'Cocoa' had died. I never did know the name of that dear old soul.

Memories of post-war Britain are memories of deprivation. A mixture of spit and salt was our only way of cleaning teeth. It was made in a saucer and applied with a damp cloth wrapped around a finger. I hated the patches that had been used to mend my worn trousers. I hated being called 'Raggy-arse!' by some other lad who did not suffer that same type of hardship which was suffered by so many young lads. I must admit to some tantalising of my younger brothers if I managed to be the one to whom mother allocated a pair of second-hand trousers.

Class distinction was something about which I learned at a very early age. Gone was that close-knit cameraderie of the war years as people began to argue over rationing. I began to learn about the power of money. Accusations of underhand and profitable dealings came out into the open. 'Yes, you bastard! We know all about the extra rations that you got with your f------money,' and then, 'These poor bairns went without bread because of bastards like you getting two loaves at a time!' It was by listening to adults that we learned of class divisions and unfair practices — we carried the class war to the rich. It became the norm for us poorer lads to attack the college cads. Poor lads, they did not choose their life-style.

One place that served as a playground for many lads after the end of the war was the old bomb-wrecked building known as Shell-Mex. This large bombed building stood at the end of the street in which we had lived with our grandmother during the war years, opposite the old and decayed Blundell's/Pointer's Yard. My boyhood memories become even more clear when recalling the late 1940s. The Shell-Mex building offered a source of fuel for hard-up folk who could not afford to buy coal or cinders from a merchant. The floors of the building were covered with small oblong logs which had been held in place with a tar-like substance. Those small logs burned very well. Enterprising youngsters filled shopping bags with the tarry logs and sold them for a few coppers. There were not many families who could afford to buy coal *and* food, so the small bags of logs were eagerly snapped up.

The wrecked Shell-Mex building provided a playground for adventurous young lads who liked to climb. All the stairs of the building were intact but the landings were wrecked. Young lads would jump from the top of a staircase and into a room — jumping back again was not so easy! How does one judge a leap from a solid surface to a crumbling piece of stair? Most just jumped the gap and threw themselves towards the wall as they landed. There were a few broken legs or ankles sustained by the daring lads who leapt through space! I was one of those lads who got hold of the remains of what had been the wooden beams of a floor and then gradually spanned the gap. There was a negro we called 'Itchycoo', a vagrant who slept amid the rubble. I remember how I would keep my distance from him, for I was still not used to the black-skinned people who were appearing on our streets.

Itchycoo died in the Shell-Mex building during the winter of 1948. It was said that attempts to remove the boots from the feet of the dead vagrant had resulted in his feet leaving his ankles because of gangrene. I joined other young lads in a morbid search for the feet which we imagined would have been left behind. How the old man had slept in the Shell-Mex building I just cannot imagine. Three inches of water covered the floor, and there were water leaks that sprung from pipes that were attached to the walls. Disturbing the stagnant pools would cause a foul and feverish smell to percolate the fusty atmosphere of damp plaster. As the foul smell arose to attack my nostrils I would hold my breath and leave the wrecked building. I called the smell 'fever' and imagined that I would fall ill with a fever if I breathed in the stagnant air.

When there were no tarry logs available as fuel for hard-up families who could not afford coal or logs from a merchant, doors would be removed from the upstairs rooms of dwelling houses and broken up for burning. Skirting boards would be removed and burned and an old couch would cover the gap so that a landlord was unaware of the destruction of his property. Some families were not frightened off by the thought of what a landlord might do. Those people removed downstairs doors from both cupboards and rooms! Many houses had curtains or old blankets where doors had once been. The curtains and the blankets were carried upstairs at night and replaced on the beds from which they had been borrowed. Floorboards would be removed from those parts of the floor where people did not walk. Legs were removed from chairs so that fires could be kept burning, and the remainder of a chair would be balanced on an empty biscuit tin. Yes, indeed; those years that followed the end of WWII were hard times.

Social security was known as the National Assistance Board, NAB for short. Old men who were still steeped in Means Test policies would order people to sell everything that they did not consider to be essential. A radio was classed as a luxury and had to be sold. Help was only given to those people who could convince the authorities that there were no saleable items in the home. Any assistance given would be minimal, and there was no assistance given for single people living with parents. People had to hide a radio or an old gramophone before a visitor from the NAB called. Because pans and kettles were heated over open fires they were subject to much burning. I remember how families had to buy washers to put into the holes. It was necessary for most folk to sleep with their clothing on during the cold months of winter. My brothers and I would huddle together as the winds blew through ill-fitting windows causing draughts in our bedroom. As we huddled together trying to keep warm, Father was buying yet another drink for some bar-room floosie as he led the life of a single and carefree man.

In later years I walked for many hours each day as I sought to keep the blood circulating through my veins during the cold days of winter. I wandered aimlessly through the streets of my home town of Hull as I awaited the nightfall that would rid me of the scornful looks of a very unsympathetic public. I was 'another bloody tramp' and 'a bloody disgrace.' My tired limbs ached as the effect of wearing wet clothing took its punishing toll, and my feet moved in a slow dragging motion as they ploughed through the dirty wet slush that had been crisp white snow just hours ago.

The holes in my shoes allowed the dirty wet slush to soak into my blistered feet, and the sodden skin became white and wrinkled like hands that have been soaked in water for too long. The wet and pulpy skin became cracked and sore, and I winced with pain as yet another piece of sodden skin came away from the top of a toe. I would be drawn towards places that had been a part of my boyhood, and I recall my great disappointment as I entered the area in which Wawne Street School had stood. Gone were those streets from which I had collected the tar that made my 'tarogs' when I had no glass marbles. Gone was that small shop where I would buy and swap secondhand comics. My boyhood had become just a memory as the tide of progress swept away the visual past. I stopped to adjust the piece of cardboard that separated my feet from the pavement — my cardboard insoles that covered the holes in the soles of my shoes.

The small corner shop that swapped the comics so many years ago was gone, but I stood for a while at that spot where it had been and visualised the counter with its piles of comics and books. 'I wish I was still a schoolboy,' I thought. I had often been told that I would change my mind about school once I was grown up. I refused to believe such nonsense, yet there I was, wishing that I was still able to swap my old Dandy or Beano comics for a copy of the Hotspur or Wizard.

Not far from the little corner shop there was another shop that had lent cycles to young lads who had a tanner to spare. The site of the little shop was now occupied by a council house. There were no more terraced homes in that area, and no more faded Union Jacks upon terraced walls. Thoughts of the old man who owned the cycle shop came to mind. The battered old cycles carried my brothers and myself for many miles as we visited the countryside or the far distant beaches of Bridlington, Scarborough, Hornsea and Withernsea. The man who owned the cycle shop was called Reggie, and any old cycle would be referred to as 'one of Reggie's grids'.

A puncture would be a common event and a nuisance. Well patched and ancient inner-tubes succumbed to the ravages of time. Makeshift repairs were made as we sought to reach our desitination. Grass from the roadside verges was used to pack the inside of tyres that held deflated, and often perished, patch-covered tubes. The grass-filled tyres were of no use when a stone or a small hole in the road was ridden over, and I can easily recall the bump, bump, bump that vibrated through the whole frame of the cycle as the valve reached the bottom position of the wheel. Pedalling a cycle with a punctured tube was hard work, and we would take turns in travelling on the bumpy conveyance.

A pleasant alternative to pedalling the many miles to the coastal resorts was visiting the countryside. My two younger brothers would join me in borrowing a grid from Reggie. Visiting the countryside was a money-making exercise as well as a pastime. Apples and brambles, gooseberries (goosegobs) and pears and strawberries were all obtained as we raided gardens. Pocket money would be made by selling our ill-gotten gains to neighbours.

I remember those irate owners of raided gardens attempting to catch us by attacking from two sides. One person would run around the house to cut off our retreat. Having been caught by one man, I was given a thick ear and my ill-gotten gains were confiscated. I looked at the man and said, 'Mr — I can't climb over the wall — will you give me leg up?' The man grabbed hold of me by the neck and said, 'You scruffy little bastard!' He then kicked my arse as he held me and I was pushed against the high wall. 'I should knock you through the bloody wall,' he said. He then put two hands together to form a cradle and said, 'Put your foot in there.' I was thrown over the wall! 'Did he hurt you?' asked my brother, Jimmy. 'No, but the twat didn't half catapult me over the bloody wall!' I replied.

Visits to the countryside involved walking along the banks of the River Hull, and I remember how I would be fascinated by the collections of straw that swirled in the waters as they travelled with the tide. Watching the small eddies would sometimes make me feel quite dizzy. I would suffer that same type of disorientation that one suffers after a long spell of looking from the window of a moving train. My brother Michael never ceased to be the adventurous one. On one of those very rare occasions when he accompanied us younger lads, Michael saw a goat in a field and decided to milk it!

I cannot recall thoughts of the adventurous Michael without also recalling domestic violence. Memories of strict discipline and sadism to which I and my brothers had been subjected as a child were often recalled during my days as a National Serviceman. More than one loud-mouthed NCO became the object of my hatred as he emulated the posturing, vicious, and domineering little ex-Lance Corporal who ruled my family home. Unpleasant memories rekindled by some bull-necked idiot with bulging eyes and a big mouth, I would lie awake at night and recall some of those violent scenes which had been so much a part of my turbulent childhood. The sound of furniture being hastily moved as Mother sought to escape the violence which a drunken animal tried to inflict upon her. The futile plea, 'Don't hit me in the face again, please — don't!' The sound of a fist as it connected with the soft flesh of Mother's face; the sound of furniture being moved as mother sought to escape the violent onslaught. My heart would be pounding with fear as I sat upon the top step of the stair. 'Please, God, start another war so that he will go away.' Foul accusations spewed forth from the slavering mouth. Accusation were made that Michael was not his child.

How well I remember those nights of violence when four very frightened young boys were crouching in the darkness at the top of the stairs. A scream of terror made us look at each other in the gloom, wondering who dare lead the way down those darkened stairs. A sudden movement by one of us would motivate the other three into action. A blind-panic run down the darkened stairs, a crashing opening of the living-room door and a dash into the room that contained an animal and a woman who was bleeding from the mouth. Brave Michael pounded his small fists against the slavering man as we younger ones ran towards our swollen-faced mother and pleaded, 'Run away, mam!'

The false accusations against Mother became a weekly ritual. Father would spend quite some time preening himself in front of the mirror before going for a night out. I do not know how that man had the nerve to give poor Mother a kiss on her cheek before he went out philandering, but he did. A few hours after the well-preened and egotistical little man had left the house, a foul-mouthed bastard would return. Bloodshot eyes, curled upper lip, flared nostrils, a sneering look. Violence was just minutes away.

Mother became quite an expert in the use of cosmetic camouflage on her blackened eyes and bruised chin as 'Gentleman Jim' was buying drinks for some floosie in a downtown bar. As Father spent money on his acquaintances poor Mother was scraping a piece of pink chalk to make powder. Some very violent arguments would be the result of Father being 'forced' to take Mother out for an evening after his cronies had expressed the desire to meet her.

I hated those very rare occasions for they always resulted in bloodshed, violence and terror. My brothers and I would once again be huddled together at the top of the stairs, and once again we would run down those stairs as we feared that poor Mother was going to be murdered by the beast. The bloodshot and bleary eyes of the drunken animal would turn in the direction of us frightened children and profanities would spew forth from the slackened, spittle-drooling lips. Mother would plead, 'Leave the bairns alone, you cruel sod. Can't you see that they are terrified?' Lying alone in the darkness, listening to the sounds of violence, tip-toeing from my room in the attic as I went to the room in which my brothers slept — when possible. I do not have any pleasant memories that are associated with my father, but I do derive some pleasure as I recall a certain incident that was not very pleasant for the master.

It was a memorable occasion when Father was confronted with absolute proof of his infidelity. A poor woman had fallen for the charms of the handsome Lothario, and was well and truly taken in by his false promises. Father had told many women of his impending divorce, and the well-worn statement, 'My wife doesn't understand me,' might have been coined by Father! I remember quite well how a knock upon the front door of our home brought to light Father's latest affair. Mother answered the door. 'Is Jimmy in?' enquired the young female caller. Mother knew that she was another victim of innocent love. 'Come on in, love,' said Mother, and she led the unsuspecting female to her lover! 'There he is, love,' said Mother, and then, 'I'm the wife who doesn't understand him, and these are his children.'

"How dare you come to my home?' Father asked. The dream of walking down the aisle with her lover was shattered. Mother said, 'Don't be too upset, love, you are not the first and you will not be the last to be duped by him.' Father attempted to dismiss the young woman and placate Mother as he said, 'You little slut! You are not fit to lick my wife's shoes.' The young woman looked shocked, as well she might at such a statement by Father. 'But you said you loved me,' she sobbed. Mother was not harsh upon the poor young woman, 'Look, love, you go home and forget about him, he's never going to alter from what he is.' The wide-eyed and ashen-faced profligate widened his nostrils, and that was a sure sign that he was very angry. The young and very distraught woman left the house in tears.

Quite a large amount of cooking had to be done over an open fire, for we did not always have money for a gas pre-payment meter. All families in our area cooked over open fires, and, because there were not many pans that had a lid to them, we often ate sooty-tasting food. I remember how the dumplings that floated on the top of a large pan got covered with soot during a soot-fall, and how I took my turn at watching the pot, which meant stirring the stew and removing the soot that fell into the pan. It is rather strange how memories of hardship and poverty can bring about nostalgia. I cherish some of those far distant days as I recall how I would watch the lighted sparks of ignited soot etching pictures. The soot at the back of a fireplace would catch a spark from the fire, and that spark would ignite more soot. The lighted soot would etch out fiery drawings at the rear of the chimney, and superstition had it that, if a face appeared in the drawing . . . someone was about to die.

It is many years since I felt the warmth of a glowing coal fire, for most new homes are fitted with electric fires only. I remember how bread was toasted before the open fire, and how my face would be glowing red if I had been given the task of toasting bread for the family meal of beans on toast. I would wrap a bit of cloth around my hand so that the fire did not burn me as I held the bread in front of the fire. We did not have a toasting fork but used a small dining fork which meant that hands were very close to the glowing embers. It may be my imagination, but I swear that bread toasted in my electric toaster does not taste the same as fire-toasted bread.

There is a strange mixture of amusement and sadness as I recall those days. Boys would shuffle to school wearing a pair of their mother's shoes that had the heels removed. Boys wore the top half of a two-piece costume that had been well worn by a sister or a mother, or they wore a tattered pair of long trousers which had been discarded by their father and which were tied at the waist with a piece of old string. Trouser bottoms were turned up many times so that they did not trail on the floor and some proud young lad told his pals. 'I've dropped,' meaning that he was now out of short pants. 'Dropping' was a very important part of growing up, and I well remember how embarrassing it was to be wearing short trousers after my voice had broken! My first pair of long trousers came from a jumble sale. Twenty-two-inch trousers bottoms became more like twenty-four-inch as quite a large amount of material was removed from the trouser legs. The waist of the trousers was very wide and almost reached my armpits. I could just manage to reach the bottoms of the very deep pockets. I felt very proud, though, as I made my first appearance at school wearing my long pants. Some snotty-nosed rich kid said, 'Ooh! aren't they baggy at the back! and then grabbed a handful of the very slack material. Any mention of blue pinstripe suits reminds me of that first pair of long pants, and of how I felt as though I had a fifty-guinea suit as I tucked my jacket sleeves inwards so that my hands could be seen.

Short haircuts were a way of keeping control of the spread of head-lice. Large blue patches on scalps would indicate a scabious condition of the head, and, because of a poor diet during the years of the war, there was very little resistance to infection. Even the smallest of cuts would turn septic, and so all schools had a period which was known as clinic time. Young lads and lasses would make their own way to the school clinic for treatment for scabs and lice, and for the extraction of teeth that had gone bad.

I remember one incident that took place at the school clinic when I was suffering from head lice. A young nurse poured lice killer onto my head, and a surplus of the mixture ran down my forehead and into my eyes. I was not given an eyebath to relieve the stinging sensation and so ran home in great pain. Father had already returned home and was on his demob leave. I remember his uniform of the Royal Welsh Fusiliers which he still wore as he awaited the issue of his pinstriped demob suit. He took me to the nearby school clinic and demanded to see the nurse who had caused me so much suffering and that she bathe my eyes. Such actions must have been taken to feed his ego, for I doubt that they were taken out of fatherly love and concern.

My father's bush hat (of the Royal Welsh Fusiliers) and the kukri knife that he brought home as a souvenir, and which he kept under his pillow are still within our family. I remember how, as a very inquisitive young lad, I drew the knife from its scabbard and cut my fingers. I dared not complain of my injury, for to have done so would have been to admit that I had dared to enter the bedroom of the master without permission. Father brought home many sovenirs of his service days in India and Burma, including a box of Turkish Delights. The square jellied sweets were cut in half by Father who said, 'You are not having a full one each, you greedy bastards.' He was addressing my brothers and me. I can only remember one occasion when he allowed himself to be pleasant to his sons. Mother had accused him of treating us lads like animals and strangers, and Father, on just that one occasion, sat me on his knee and rubbed his stubble-covered chin against mine.

Although my father only gave a small amount of money to Mother for housekeeping, he was not an idle man. When work was difficult to find for our men who returned home after the war, he decided to have a go at setting himself up in a painting and decorating capacity. A small loan from SAAFA enabled him to purchase the basic equipment needed, and so J. F. Bromby, Painter and Paper-hanger, became a business man. The most ridiculous thing he did was to have some small business cards printed and give those cards to people he knew in the pub.

We were used to move decorating materials to the place of work. A bicycle had a plank of wood strapped along its length and a pair of steps tied to the handlebars. Pots of paint hung from the loaded cycle. I did my share of pushing the loaded cycle for many miles to the place of work. My brothers and myself would take turns in pushing the cycle and carrying rolls of wallpaper. Young muscles ached as we swapped tasks during the many miles of walking. The loaded cycle had to be lifted when changing direction, for the plank and steps prevented steering.

I have painted many fences and many doors with undercoat, and I have pasted countless rolls of wallpaper. The end of each working day meant that I had to wash out the brushes with turps, and scrub the pasting board, and clean the paste bucket. If I was not on holidays from school then I would have to go to the place of work after school had finished for the day and carry out my duties. I did not have much time for boyhood pursuits if Father had work to do. The largest amount of money that I ever received was ten shillings (50p). I was not to have the benefit of spending money as Father said, 'Now give me that money back so that I can invest it for you,' and he then gave me a two shilling (10p) piece and said, 'I'll invest the money in brewery shares for you.'

When Father was unable to obtain enough work to maintain his business, he dismissed any worries that Mother expressed and went into partnership — and towards the termination of his venture into the world of the self-employed. Life with Father after the collapse of his business became even worse than it already was. It became a real Hell on earth as the little tyrant blamed everyone but himself.

Never a one for idleness, Father entered into a government training scheme. His innermost thoughts were always close to the surface, and after a few pints of beer in a nearby public house he vented his anger on his family.

One of the most fearful punishments which was meted out by father was one which he devised during the dark nights of the winter months of around the year 1947. I remember how he often expressed the desire to be able to think of the ultimate punishment. One method he used was introduced after I expressed my fear of the darkness. There were no light fittings in our home during the late Forties. Gas lighting was the only means of illumination in most homes. Father already knew that I feared the darkness when he sent me to my attic room alone, and, as I climbed the flights of stairs to the attic he said, 'Off you go to your nice dark attic and the man who is waiting there in the darkness.' I ran my hands along the wall as a guide in the darkness, and I shuddered as I passed the small passage that led to the rear upstairs room. My breathing was fast and my heart was pounding. Stars appeared before my eyes as I peered into the gloom. I reached the smaller staircase that led into the attic. Dark shapes appeared to be moving in the darkness, and I imagined some evil being lurking in that passage which led to the rear room . . . I turned around, I stumbled, I grabbed the bannister. I half fell and half ran as I descended the darkened stairs and burst into the living room . . . 'I'm frightened!' I blurted out amid my tears. My breathing was laboured as I begged to be allowed to wait until the other lads were ready for bed. My heart pounded even more as I saw the look of anger on the face of the master who was leaping from his fireside chair. A curled lip, a fierce stare. Rough and violent hands grabbing me and bruising my flesh as I sought to escape his wrath. Mother begged him to let me go . . . 'You're hurting the bairn!' she shouted as she begged for mercy on my behalf. 'I know how to deal with insubordination from this bastard!' said father. I was roughly pushed towards the stairs and told, 'Get back up those stairs, and don't you dare to make another bloody sound.' I screamed with terror as I was pushed towards the darkness with Father uttering the words. I ran up the stairs as fast as my hands and feet would allow me to. I reached the small dark attic room and fumbled my way through the inky black darkness towards my bed.

My shins knocked against the iron frame of my bed as I leapt beneath the covers. The darkness of the attic was indeed a punishment as I lay beneath the sparse covers. My breathing became the breathing of someone else. I held my breath . . . Yes! there was someone else in the room. Did I just feel a hand touch me? Bright lights swam before my eyes and my heart almost burst from my chest. I leapt from my bed and once more dashed down the stairs in fear. Tears ran down my cheeks as I ran into the living room and screamed the words, 'I hate you!' and then, as I stared at the animal who was inflicting punishment upon me, I said, 'I'm going to kill you when I grow big and strong!' I was grasped by the short hairs at the nape of my kneck as my sire steered me towards a small dark cupboard. As I was thrown I was told, 'There are plenty of spiders to keep you company in there!' I crouched inside the cupboard that had once been a shelter from the German bombers. I was taken from it some time later and given a beating by Father as he said, 'I am the master — you will always obey me.'

Happier memories of my childhood return to me some evenings as I sit reflecting on a life that has been so badly affected by alcohol and violence. Those pleasant memories of daring young lads who would hang from the tailboard of a cart that was being pulled by a horse. Drivers of the carts would be aware that we were stealing a ride, but the drivers were not always able to catch us. By the time a driver had jumped from his seat and made his way to the back of the cart we would be gone. Longer whips were to be introduced by some drivers, and I well remember how happy I was as I snatched a free ride and thought that the driver of the cart did not know that I was there. Crack went the long whip, and I felt a stinging sensation on my face.

One of the saddest faces I have ever seen was that of a coal merchant who delivered to the homes near to the Wawne Street School. I was having a snowball fight with some other lads during the winter of 1950. The ill-fated horse of the coal merchant slipped on the hard, icy ground. As a crowd gathered around the fallen horse, many hands were put to the task of attempting to assist the poor creature to its feet. All the efforts of young boys and men and women were to no avail. The poor creature had broken a leg. The harness was removed from the stricken creature as it lay snorting out great clouds of steaming breath from its huge nostrils, breath that froze in the thin, cold air. A small van arrived on the scene and a man from the RSPCA alighted carrying a small tube and a hammer. The tube turned out to be a humane killer.

I did not associate the humane killer with a gun, and so I was startled when the man placed the tube to the head of the animal and struck the end. Bang! Blood gushed forth from the head of the horse. That huge and magnificent head that had so often turned with impatience was now stilled. The body of the horse shook as the last exhalation of breath took place. The huge muscular legs made jerky movements as the throes of death signalled the end of life. All was still just a few minutes after the shot was fired. A large fat lady came into the scene carrying a bucket of water and a stiff sweeping brush. Blood that had stained the road and flowed along the gutter was swilled and swept away, but not before red rivulets had been formed in the white snow. Those red rivulets of blood matched the white streaks that were etched into the coal-blackened face of the grieving merchant as tears fell down a cheek. The coal merchant was not alone in his grief, for my schoolfriends and myself were also crying over the death of the poor unfortunate horse.

Happiness was to replace sadness when two old men entered upon the tragic scene. They were buskers who lived nearby to the scene of the tragedy. One of the buskers was confined to a wheelchair. He played the knick-knacks, two pieces of flat bone that were rattled together. His companion played the banjo. I tried many times to master the technique of playing the knick-knacks but without any success. If any of us had a spare farthing we would give it to the buskers. It is 40 years ago since I stood watching and listening as the two buskers entertained passers by, and yet it seems like just a short time ago that I watched the little player of the knick-knacks as he danced around the wheel chair of his dark-skinned and crippled companion.

Chapter Four
A MISSPENT YOUTH

Shortly after my father had returned home after the end of WWII, Mother fell pregnant. Like the selfish creature that he was, Father told Mother to get rid of the fertilized foetus, 'Get rid of it. I've enough on my plate with these bastards!' said Father. Mother was bullied into attempts to induce menstruation: threats of violence and abandonment led her into drinking a substance known as Red Lavender which was boiled and consumed when it was as hot as it was possible for the mouth to bear.

I recall one occasion when Father attempted to induce an abortion by ramming his fist into the unprotected stomach of Mother. 'I told you to get rid of it!' he screamed. As Mother protested that she had tried and failed, Father leapt out of his chair and shouted, 'Perhaps this will get rid of the bastard!' and it was then that he punched her stomach. The wind was driven from the lungs of poor Mother as that evil, vile, corrupt and vicious animal unleashed his murderous assault upon the unborn foetus and upon Mother. His vile actions did not get rid of it and 'It' was born and christened Geoffrey, the first of four more sons that Mother would bear and give birth to. She bore others for a while before Father made sure that the pregnancy was terminated. On one occasion when mother had brought about menstruation by drinking Red Lavender she was alone in the house when the child (or foetus) began to come away. It was not very often that Mother had a visit from Grandmother, but she decided to visit just at the time when Mother was lying on her bed begging for help as the well-advanced pregnancy was being terminated. Mother told me when I was older. 'I lay on the bed and cried out for Mother to help me.' The saddest thing about the episode was when Grandmother spoke the words, 'It was a girl,' and poor Mother who had always wanted a daughter wept into her pillow.

Grandmother called for the doctor to visit Mother, and as the doctor was examining her Father came home from the pub. The doctor gave Father a stern lecture about his failure to take any precautions. Father was not a Catholic; he just believed that women should always be tied to the home with plenty to keep them occupied, and he also enjoyed the pleasure of unprotected sex. Precautions were only for extra-marital affairs as far as he was concerned.

One happy story is of the early morning market held on the Corporation Field, a huge concreted area of land that was also used for the horse show each year. I would rise early when the morning market had taken place, and visit the site where the stalls had been set. Carrots and potatoes were left behind after the market men had gone, as was rotten fruit, cabbage leaves and tomatoes, bad apples and damaged fruit. All made good eating for a lad who wanted to spend his school dinner money on cigarettes!

Another misuse of dinner money was to buy a bowl of pea soup and two loose cigarettes. One of the cigarettes was given to any girl who would be prepared to do some heavy petting. As I became a spotty faced teenager I became very shy. The few times that I had indulged in immature sexual practices with some of my female friends counted for nothing as I began to mature. I was not to experience adult sex until I was a young soldier. My cigarette bought me a few kisses and some intimate touching — no more than that.

When I was not misusing my school dinner money I enjoyed a good wholesome meal. I enjoyed all my school meals, and I could never understand those lads who called the meals horrible. I think that perhaps they had never suffered want. During the summer holidays dinners were served on the production of a green ticket. If Father was not working, or if he was earning a low wage, a free dinner would be made available to us. Free milk was also given to poor families. My hatred of the rich was increased as boys from the better-off families would shout abuse and taunts. I enjoyed the company of those children who had patches in their pants and holes in their shoes. They were my kind of people. Perhaps some of those raggy-arsed kids grew up to be some of the men with whom I shared a bottle as I sat on some roadside bench. I don't know.

The courting of girls during my early teens was something that I sadly missed out on. I was very conscious of my raggy pants even though those pants had been neatly patched by my mother. Patched pants were very embarrassing to a teenager. I spent a lot of time standing with my back to the wall as I stood in the playground. If I did take a walk with a girl I would always stay one step behind so as to prevent her from seeing my patched trousers. A mixture of shame and shyness prevented me from seeking a serious relationship with any of the girls that I liked and lusted after.   I was aged 14 before I was able to hold my head high with the pride of wearing a new suit. Hire purchase and credit sales were being made easier for hard-up families, and I was at last able to have some new clothes and shoes instead of hand-me-downs and jumble sale bargains. I remember how I took my first club-check to the Northern outfitters and obtained new shoes and socks, a new suit and a tie, and underwear. I had never worn a pair of underpants before. Only Father could afford to dress correctly in our house. I was constantly pressing my new trousers and polishing my shoes. I was not used to wearing a pair of shoes, for my father insisted that my brothers and

I wore well-studded boots. We had the regulation army-style 13 studs in each sole of our boots.

The credit sales system boomed. Young girls who had been Cinderella lookalikes were transformed overnight into princesses. Girls who had not looked very attractive in old clothing were fighting off many suitors when they arrived at school looking like models. I was very self-conscious about my skinny build and so dared not ask a really beautiful girl for a date. I became very aware of my lack of stature when I asked one beauty for a date after taking quite some time to pluck up the courage to do so. The answer I was given was, 'When you have grown a bit I might.' I sent for information about a course of body-building by Charles Atlas but I could not afford the course and so held on to what small amount of cash I did have. I hoped that I would be able to spend my few shillings on taking a girl to the pictures. I did take one rather fat girl to the pictures and she asked me to marry her! Perhaps she thought that marriage was the decent thing after I had touched her stocking tops in the darkness of the cinema, and she had tried to push her tongue into my mouth. I had reeled back when she tried that.

I was in my final year of schooling during 1952 and I was being taught in a mixed class, a real treat! How exciting it was to be in a desk next to a girl who I thought was very nice looking. She was named Doreen and her eyes matched her surname. Lovely dark brown eyes set in a very nice face. The lovely Doreen did not receive all my admiration. Joan was also very beautiful, and had a large dimple in her chin. I eventually managed to make friends with a couple of girls who were as shy as me. We talked a lot about 'It' but never got around to doing 'It'. Shyness prevented us from exploring the delights of the flesh. Victorian teachings about sexual behaviour prevented most girls from going any further than touching. I was at that age when boys got very hot and bothered when kissing a girl.

It was not only because of sexual development that I became frustrated during my youth. The self-loving and arrogant tyrant in our home saw his growing sons as rivals. I was far too interested in those lovely teenage girls, and could not have cared less about the master. There was enough trouble in our home already.

As the time approached when I would finish my schooling I was ordered to write after a job as an apprentice engineer. A firm from Wolverhampton, the Hull Gauge and Tool Company, was about to open a branch in Hull. I wrote for an interview and was given a job to start after the Easter holiday, 1952. I obtained a club check so that I could purchase overalls and working boots.

My first day at work was really exciting, and just donning my overalls made me feel very important. I was a grown up! I made tea for the men at my place of work, I swept the floor, I cleaned the machines, I queued for the fish and chips at dinner time, and I cleaned the boss's car. 'When do I start engineering?' I asked of the foreman. 'All in good time, lad, all in good time,' said the man. I pulled a barrow filled with castings, and I helped the boss as he patched the exhaust of his car. Father had just finished a six-month course at the Remploy training centre. He had been working on a milling machine and I was asked to approach my boss on his behalf to see if there was a vacancy — and so my place of work was no longer a place of sanctuary. Father began working as a turner.

Shortly after, I had an accident with a drilling machine. My hair got caught and was ripped from my scalp. Far from complaining that there were no safety guards on the machines and drills, Father called me a clumsy and useless idiot! He thought more about his good relationship with the boss, who had turned out to be one of his school chums.

There were many cast iron components used at my place of work, and it was my job to visit the nearby foundry to collect the castings. I was quite surprised to see a woman working in the foundry. A man told me that the woman had started her job on a temporary basis during the war years. Lots of women had taken on jobs that were normally done by men. When fighting men returned after the war most women returned to being housewives. Returning soldiers soon began the spawning of a new generation to replace that which lay buried in some foreign field.

My wages at the engineering firm were very low, £1.10s [£1.50], and as an apprentice I was expected to do seven years before I could claim a full wage. I was not happy with the wage, I was not happy about being a general dogsbody, I was not at all happy about the fact that I had a bald patch after the accident with the drill, and I was most definitely not happy working alongside my father. My friends were earning twice my wage as errand boys. When I saw a job of errand boy advertised at £2.50 I applied for it. Father was not very pleased with my decision to leave the engineering trade, and I was warned that if I dared to leave my new place of employ I would be thrown out of the home. I had made a good move, for the small leather merchants' firm which I joined was a one big happy family business. I enjoyed the work and soon got to know my shoe repairers by their Christian names. I was eventually promoted to work behind the counter, and I stayed with that firm until I was made redundant in 1958.

Still aged 15, and installed into my new job, I visited my grandmother who lived just a short distance away from our home. It was after visiting my 'Nanny', as she preferred to be called, that I noticed one of my cousins in a nearby yard. I walked over to say hello. There was a snooker table set up in the yard and my cousin Stan was playing a frame with the proud owner of the table — a lad named Ron. I asked if I could join them and learn how to play. As I joined them I little realised that that day was to shape my future for many years to come. I struck up a good friendship with Ron, and we spent many hours at the snooker table. I got to know his family quite well, and each Saturday would become a real treat for me when I was asked to join them for dinner. Ron had an elder brother and three sisters. Ron told me that his sister Maureen was very moody. He was speaking about my future wife.

Learning to play snooker was a great time for me for I enjoy any game that is not strenuous but which is competitive. I would join Ron and my cousin Stan when they went to the cinema or the theatre. I enjoyed the theatre, and remember seeing such famous acts as Roy Hudd, Ken Dodd, Fred Karno's Army and George Formby. I went to see Arthur (Old Mother Riley) Lucan one evening but only saw his understudy, for Mr Lucan had become ill. I enjoyed watching the long-legged chorus girls dancing on stage and, just as I had fancied the girls who had got me frustrated on the fairground stalls, I also fancied the girls in the chorus line. Ron and I would pick out our best choice of the girls on stage.

I was aged 17 when I bought my first bottle of ale at the Palace Theatre bar. The small bottle contained Hull Brewery Amber. I enjoyed the taste of the light coloured liquid Amber — there was life outside the institution that I called home. I was on the threshold of a whole new episode of my life. I was able to start enjoying life as I followed new pursuits, oblivious of the fact that my new-found freedom and enjoyment was soon to come to an end.

I was nearing the age of conscription and further dominance from tyrannical corporals. My friendship with Ron became action-packed. We enjoyed shooting air pistols and air rifles, we both enjoyed snooker and darts. Girls were a part of our lives that left us both feeling frustrated with ourselves. My air pistol took away my frustration as I shot at very small targets and hit them. I became obsessed with perfection. I had noticed that, after drinking a couple of small bottles of ale at the theatre, I became more confident. I tried drinking a bottle of cider and liked it. I would pretend to be drunk as I asked a girl for a kiss, and I thought that drinking cider would impress the girls with whom Ron and I had become acquainted. I did not find those girls as attractive as the very lovely Miss Brown who had made my pulse race in the classroom, but I did enjoy kissing them and wishing that I could go further. I was a growing lad in more ways than just my height. Having already acquired a taste for alcohol I began to wonder what it would be like to drink in a public house. I asked Ron if he would dare to accompany me into a pub. The chosen pub (now demolished) was the Stag Inn in Leonard Street.

Two very hesitant young lads entered the side door of the pub and sat down in the smoke room. 'Yes, lads, what'll it be?' asked the landlord. 'Er, two pints of mild, please,' I said. The two huge glasses of beer were placed in front of two novice ale consumers. I thought that the pints were going to be too much to consume, for I imagined that beer in a pub was far stronger than other beer or cider. My entry into the public house marked the beginning of an addiction which would shatter the lives of many people, and which would eventually lead me into vagrancy.

Both Ron and myself were violently sick after managing to consume two pints of beer each. I heaved and balked my way to a piece of waste land. My head was swimming as I heaved up yet again. I suppose the sensible thing to do after such an unpleasant experience is to say, 'Never again,' and mean it. The world is filled with lots of people who drink again after a bad experience. Well, they can't allow people to accuse them of not being able to take it, can they?

Just two nights after my bad experience of drunkenness, I repeated the whole process over again. Two pints, some fresh air, feel dizzy and then vomit. After just a few more visits to the pub I was able to drink four pints without vomiting.

Lack of finances prevented me from visiting the pub more than twice each week, but a greater curtailment of my consumption of alcohol came via a long brown envelope which bore the four letters OHMS. I opened the official envelope. 'Dear Mr Bromby,' the letter began. I was instructed to attend an army medical centre. I was about to lose my freedom, I was about to undergo more of that type of discipline that had been so much a part of my childhood and boyhood.

'Cough, please,' said the man who had his hand on my scrotum. A gentle squeeze of a cold hand felt for some reaction as I gave an embarrassed, 'Ahem.' A quick test for colour blindness and a sham of an examination. A silly test of co-ordination that even a five-year-old could have passed, and that was it.

A few weeks after my examination I received another of those OHMS letters. I was to report to the Victoria Barracks, Beverley. There was a visitor to our home, my cousin Alan who had come to see if I had been called up to the same unit as he had been told to report to. Yes, we were both to report to the Victoria Barracks. It was good to have someone going with me into the great unknown. It was a fine day in August, 1955. I said my farewell to Mother and left the house with my cousin. My belongings were in a paper carrier bag. I had just a few shillings in my pocket.

There were quite a few young men waiting in Paragon Station, and in answer to the question, 'Are you going to Victoria Barracks?' they all replied, 'Yes.' There were no happy faces that I can recall. The gathering together of us pimply faced young men was the beginning of a spirit of togetherness. We were all about to 'get some in'. There was some speculation as to what army life would be like. I was more than able to give the lads some idea of what to expect. I drew on my experience of life with a vicious little ex-lance-corporal.

Chapter Five

ARMY LIFE BEGINS

Someone noticed the arrival of two men in army uniform. 'Oh, well,' said one lad. 'This is it. They have come to get us.' A corporal came towards us apprehensive young lads. 'Right, then, who wants a nice ride to their new home?' I didn't like his attitude.

A small board held in the hand of the corporal contained a list of the names of lads who should be present. 'Answer when your name is called,' said the corporal. I was reminded of home when one of the corporals said, 'Come on, get in line, look as though you are alive!' Other lads had not been used to being ordered about. 'Who the f---does this twat think he is?' asked one of the lads. 'When I call out your name I want you to answer with an affirmative!' said the corporal with the roster. 'What the f---is an affirmative?' asked one lad of another. 'Just say you are present,' said another lad. 'Why the hell didn't he just say that?'retorted the other. I was stifling my laughter as I marvelled at those lads who treated authority as though it were nothing. I did not like the look of the lance-corporal who accompanied the full corporal. Corporal P was a small man with a little black moustache, and I soon found out that he was not a bad chap. His bark was worse than his bite. Corporal G was a different type; he imagined himself to be important. Corporal P said, 'Never address me as, Hey you! Always address me as Corporal.'

Having completed the roll call we were ushered out of the railway station to a three-ton army wagon. 'Rookies', 'Sprags', and other names were used to describe us lads during our ten weeks of intensive training. Army life is not for the faint-hearts or the Puritans! Once aboard the truck, the tailboard was lifted into place and the two securing pins fastened. 'A tailboard like this one fell on a young lass and killed her,' I remarked. How strange that something as simple as a pin being put into place could revive such a sad memory.

The army barracks were only a few minutes drive away from the station. I disliked being in the back of the moving vehicle, unable to see where I was going (during my time as a long-distance driver in 1970 I never slept in the back of the vehicle when being relieved by my co-driver). I was pleased when the short journey to the Victoria Barracks was over. As I looked out from the back of the vehicle I saw a barrier being lowered by the man who was guarding the gate. He shouted towards the wagon and us 'sprogs,' 'You're going to f------love it here!' He then gave a laugh which indicated sarcasm. We were all sitting quietly, and only one voice retorted, rudely but very quietly.

The wagon came to a halt and Corporal P appeared and removed the holding pins from the tailboard. 'Come on, you lot, let's have you out!' he commanded. I jumped from the high floor of the vehicle and my feet landed on army territory. I cannot recall much about that first day as a young conscript, but one very vivid memory remains. As my name was called out I answered and was told that I would be in Ypres platoon. My cousin Alan answered his name. 'Ypres platoon,' said the corporal. I sighed with relief. Other lads looked happy as they were designated to the same platoon as someone with whom they had struck up an acquaintance during the journey from Hull. The old Victoria Barracks had just received some more raw recruits who were to sweat and curse for a period of ten weeks — young men who would march over a cliff if they were ordered to do so once their training was finished. Swearing did not bother me at all. It was just as well that it didn't, for army life is incomplete without it. Men who are trained to kill do not indulge in the niceties of etiquette.

After we had been told which platoon we were to be in, we were taken to the stores to draw our kit and a lecture about the responsibility for the kit was given as we entered. Collecting it was a straight-forward affair. 'Hold out your arms, palms upwards,' said the corporal in charge. As we moved along a counter, kit was piled into the outstretched arms. My outstretched arms were loaded with — 'Caps six and seven eighths, two! Boots, black, size seven, pairs two!' and 'Helmet, steel, one!' Uniforms, boots and gaiters, webbing, shoulder flashes and 'housewife'. No, not a female to take back to our bed space — a 'housewife' was a small pouch that contained a packet of needles, some spare buttons and a reel of cotton.

'I can't see where I'm going,' I remarked as the kit in my arms blocked my vision. 'You know where you came from, laddie. Just reverse your memory!' I was told. The corporal said, 'If you drop anything, leave it until you have got rid of what you are carrying.' The advice came too late for me as I reached down to try and retrieve my fallen helmet, steel. I was not alone in my embarrassment as the whole pile fell from my arms. The conversation that followed made it home from *home*.

I was delighted that my cousin Alan was given the bed next to mine. We were able to talk of our family as we sat polishing brasses, bulling boots, and cleaning our rifles. I soon began to make conversation with some of the other lads, most of whom were pleasant enough. Just a couple of the other lads were unsociable and aggressive.

My first army meal introduced me to bromide. The tea was a darkish colour and tasted peculiar. 'That funny taste is caused by bromide,' said one knowledgeable young man, and then, 'My old man said they put it in your tea so that you will not feel frisky.' I do not know which regiment the father of that lad had trained with, but training with the East Yorks did not leave any energy or desire. Despite the fact that I was feeling tired after the end of day one, I was not able to sleep. Lots of cigarettes glowing in the darkness showed me that I was not alone with my insomnia. I suppose that I must have managed some sleep, but it seemed as though I had been awake all night as I heard my first Reveille played on an army bugle. Just seconds after the bugler had finished there was a flurry of movement in the barrack room. I was startled by the entrance of a maniac, seemingly an escapee from a mental institution who bore three stripes upon his arms. 'I'm your sergeant, I'm your mother, I'm your father!' said the madman. I disagreed inwardly that he was my mother but recognised the father claim. The madman left the barrack room as quickly as he had entered it. I did not see him again until three days later.

Day two of army life was a very sad day indeed for many young lads who had taken pride in their hairstyle. The D.A. (Ducks Arse) hairstyles were popular in the 1950s. Thick hair at the back of our head would be combed towards the centre from each side, and a comb would be run down the centre as a finishing touch. There were many glum faces as a sarcastic barber with a tape on his arm said, 'Ooh, just look at all those lovely curls falling on the floor,' and then, 'Your days of needing an oil change are over!' I was reminded of those punishment cuts that my father had given to me when I was just a young lad. The haircuts were appalling! 'Everything that fits under your cap is yours. The rest is all mine,' said the barber. We were left with just a small bit of hair on the top of our head.

I cannot remember many details of those first few days, but the crazy sergeant is easily recalled. Just a few days after the first encounter with the pompous idiot, in he came again just seconds after Reveille. I was already well trained in the art of jumping to it. The sergeant said, 'I'll be back to inspect you lot after breakfast.' Army food was always very good, but the whole process of eating was too speeded up for us young rookies to enjoy our meals. 'Come on, come on! You're here to eat food, not to natter away like a lot of silly tarts.'

I was not happy. I did not like the army. I did not like the thought of two years of rushing about at the double. I was not to know that the army proper is much easier than the army training camps. The inspection that followed breakfast each day was just an excuse to break our spirit further. I was not aware of the 'break them and make them policy', and the thought of two years of strict discipline was very disheartening.

When we were given our army numbers we were told to memorise them. It is said that a man never forgets his army number — 23169528 — and it's true! And so it was that a band of young men were to take those first steps towards uniformity. Thirty boots could crash down at the same second, but not before we had sweated and sworn and stumbled. Looking back to those days on the barrack square I feel a great sense of achievement. I did not have such feelings at the time, though. It is remarkable how a group of men can be taught how to become automatons. The initial stages of drill were a fiasco. 'Left turn, right turn, about turn.' 'Right wheel, left wheel, mark time!' What a mess!

The crazy sergeant spewed forth his abuse as young men sweated and gasped for breath. 'You may have broken your mother's heart but you will not break mine!' shouted the sergeant, and then, 'You will stay here until you get it right!' A major came on the scene. 'Let the men rest,' he said. The nutcase sergeant gave him plenty of the 'Yes, sir, no, sir, three bags full, sir.' No sooner had the major left the scene than the sergeant said, 'I'm in charge on this parade ground.'

The first introduction of music on the parade ground caused a sensation that I had never before experienced. I felt pride surging through my whole body. The feeling is a tingling sensation and is very similar to that feeling which affected me when I saw the appearance of a lovely girl who was keeping our first date. I marched to the sound of Colonel Bogey without knowing that there were words to the music — I did not hear the words until I joined the trained soldiers in Ulster.

I wrote a letter home and mentioned that there were some NCOs who were just like Father and that I felt like killing them. Poor Mother took my letter very seriously, and she wrote to the C.O. to complain about the treatment. Horror of horrors! I was glad that the other lads did not know about the letter for I would have been considered a weakling. I was taken before the major, as was the corporal about whom I had told Mother. I denied that there was any bullying, and suggested that Mother had misinterpreted my words. Corporal 'Twat' ceased to be aggressive towards me and even offered me a piece of his chocolate bar. I wrote a letter to Mother and expressed my anger at her interference which had caused me so much embarrassment. Poor Mother, she had only been trying to help.

Drill, drill, drill, and more bloody drill on the parade ground. Drill seemed to be the major part of our training. I am told that it prevents men from thinking for themselves when orders are given. A drill was deemed to be good for us after we had been given some very painful jabs. My arm felt as though it had been thumped with an iron fist, and all the other lads expressed their agony too. Despite our exertions on the square, the pain persisted. Not many lads were able to sleep that night. 'I'm gonna write ter Bessie Braddock,' said one lad. Bessie Braddock was the Labour MP who campaigned for underdogs.

Because of my love of air pistols I was already a keen shot. I had waited impatiently for the day when we would be able to fire our guns. We were informed that no guns are fired. 'You discharge your weapon!' said the sergeant in charge, and then, 'You do not fire bullets. You fire rounds.' The big day finally arrived. We were taken to a firing range.

I trembled with excitement as I took my first aim at a target. I had been told to pull the stock of the weapon well into my shoulder. My breathing seemed to shiver as I inhaled and then exhaled. My heart beat faster, and I had butterflies in my stomach. I looked at the target. 'Put the tip of the foresight into the centre of the aperture, aim, restrain breathing — and fire,' were the instructions given by the sergeant. If I had to describe my most thrilling moment, then firing my first round would be my choice. I took steady aim at the target that stood two hundred yards away. I centred my sights on the 'Bull.' My breathing was fast and my hands were trembling. I gently squeezed the trigger. The front of the rifle seemed to rise into the air as I 'followed through', and then it slowly fell again. Excitement coursed through my whole body. I could hardly wait till we had returned to barracks, so that I could put pen to paper and let my friend Ron know how it felt to fire a real gun. No one broke a shoulder by failing to hold the butt of the rifle firmly into their shoulder, but there were quite a few bruises to be seen. I was bruised, and my clavicle hurt.

The Bren-gun did not offer me as much excitement as the rifle, but I did enjoy my brief encounter with the Sten-gun. My most exciting moment on a firing range was about 18 months after I first discharged a round from my .303 Lee-Enfield, but, back to the rookie range. I qualified first class on both the Bren and the rifle. I only ever fired six rounds from a revolver, and I only ever threw two hand-grenades. I also only fired a Sten-gun once.

The throwing of grenades provided some drama. There was a small wall behind which we stood as we threw the grenade, and which we crouched behind after the grenade had been hurled towards a target area. One lad removed the pin from his grenade, and then dropped the bloody grenade at his feet! The sergeant in charge shouted, 'You clumsy bastard!' as he grabbed hold of the soldier with one hand and threw him towards the safety wall. The other hand of the fast-moving sergeant was picking up the ready-to-explode grenade and hurling it over the wall towards the range. A breathless and red-faced sergeant joined us behind the safety wall just as the grenade exploded.

During those ten weeks of training at the Victoria Barracks my feelings of patriotism were born. I learned of the history of the name of my platoon, and that of the other platoon which was training alongside us, the Somme platoon. I can never watch a poppy day ceremony without thinking of those thousands of young men who fought under such terrible conditions in all past wars.

The army taught me many things about reality. I later heard seasoned soldiers speak of cutting genitals from a dead bandit and sticking them in his mouth as he lay dead, propped against a tree. The idea of such actions is to scare his companions, and let them know that war is not a game between gentlemen. 'Strike fear into the heart of your enemy,' is the order of the day.

Bayonet practice was accompanied by screams of 'Kill the bastard!' as we attacked a suspended sack of hay. We were taught that the small groove in the bayonet was for air to enter the wound that one inflicted upon the enemy. The air prevented suction from holding the bayonet in a punctured stomach. 'Twist it as you pull it out,' said the sergeant. One lad asked what would he do if his bayonet would not come out of a stomach. 'Pull your trigger and blow the bastard out!' said the all-knowing NCO.

I could not help but laugh at some of the lads as they gave a squeaky and not very enthusiastic 'scream' as they bayonetted the sack of straw. Our instructor said to me, 'This is bloody serious, laddie, you're training to be a killer!' 'Report to me here at 1800 hours,' said the sergeant, and then, 'We'll see just how funny you think bayonet practice is after you have attacked the bag for a couple of hours!' I attacked the bag for just five minutes before the sergeant dismissed me. I was told many times over of the supremacy of the British soldier. I became proud of my heritage. One bit of information given to us was that it is an offence to polish the bayonet with metal cleaner as it could give the enemy blood-poisoning! It would be alright to rip out the man's guts or slash his throat. There are certainly some strange rules of war. I doubt that a soldier who is face-to-face with the enemy would bother about niceties or Geneva conventions. 'Never ever speak of the man before you, or think of the man before you when making a bayonet charge. You are attacking an enemy soldier who will kill you if you hesitate for just one second.' I am pleased that I never had to put my training into practice. I can imagine myself shooting the enemy, but bayonet charges are for people who are made of sterner stuff than I.

Basic training came to an end but there was more training yet to come before I could call myself a soldier and get rid of the sprog tag. The passing-out parade was an open day. Mother was unable to attend because of the need to stay at home with the (then) two youngest lads, Geoffrey and Trevor. Father chose not to come to the ceremony simply because he had no time for burdens, as we boys were called. My friend Ron came to the passing-out ceremony. I still recall the delighted look upon his face as I let him handle the .303 Lee Enfield rifle. 'Cor,' said the delighted Ron. 'This is what I call a gun!' So did I before I was told to call it a rifle or a weapon.

After the parade was over and all civilians had left the camp, we prepared for a night out at a public house. It was the custom for the sergeant or corporal in charge to take his men for a drink. In the case of Ypres platoon it was Corporal P who took us. I got hopelessly drunk and I cannot remember too much about events. I do remember that I kept repeating the words, 'Good old Smithy!' A private named Smith had taken up the challenge made by the arrogant sergeant who offered to fight on the field. Smithy said, 'I'll be on the field waiting for you.' The sergeant did not turn up. His loud-mouthed bragging had all been a sham. 'Good old Smithy,' I mumbled. Cousin Alan had to assist me as I struggled to undress for bed. I gave one more accolade to 'Good old Smithy' and then fell asleep.

The following day had us packing our kit bags as we made ready for a week's leave prior to our embarkation to Ulster. The seven days passed far too quickly as I savoured once more the delights of the public house which had become my local. Darts and dominoes and beer dominated my leave. I over-indulged with the beer and was late back at the barracks. Because we were leaving for Ireland I escaped punishment.

The journey to Liverpool was a long and tiresome one. We were cramped together in the rear of an army three-tonner (a Bedford three-ton vehicle/ Army wagon). I recall stopping for a meal at some army camp along the way, but where that camp was situated I have no idea. The huge dining area, which us soldiers called the 'mess,' looked cold and uninviting compared with the small mess-hall to which we had grown accustomed. Everything I saw filled me with great disappointment. Huge buildings that reminded me of the prisons that I had seen at the cinema when a gangster film was being shown filled me with a sense of foreboding. The atmosphere of the huge barracks was one of coldness and unhappiness. I was to be spared having to move into a cold-looking block until such time as I had become accustomed to the barracks to which us rookies were posted. We finally reached Liverpool during the evening. It was a dark November evening.

I was not looking forward to the journey by sea. I have a fear of large open spaces that are filled with water! I had a moment when my fear and apprehension left me and that was as I boarded the ferry. I thought of all those newsreel films that had been shown during the war. Those poor men who were going to fight a war were all smiles! How strange it is that such thinking was to play a very important part in my later life as I started to battle against alcoholism.

During the sea crossing from Liverpool to Belfast there were many wise-cracks as young men sought to hide their feelings of anxiety . . . 'What will the army be like?' . . . 'I'll bet it is awful being in a large barracks' etc. etc. I made the journeys home on leave and was never seasick. How strange that the final trip home had me 'Spewing my guts up.' That bout of vomiting at sea was worse than any I had experienced after a night on the booze.

[In Ireland when stationed in Londonderry he met 'a wonderful blue-eyed girl', Margaret, with whom he had a passionate affair. She was a Catholic and there were problems of religion and mixed marriage. On completion of his service he returned to Hull.]

Chapter Six

A NEW LOVE

Although I had been paid enough money to cover a week's leave after my demob from the army, I resumed work at the leather shop within two days of arriving back in Hull. My parents had moved home during that time which I had served in Ulster, and so I was to start civilian life in a home with a bath and an indoor toilet. Our new home was on one of the housing estates that were built to replace those old terraced dwellings and street dwellings that had been so much a part of my childhood. My father had met me at the station when I first arrived home from Ulster. He had borrowed a van from his place of work so that he could drive me to our new home. Well, well, well! I was being treated as an adult by the master.

As we approached the end of our journey Father said, 'There is a good social club just up the road — I'll take you there tonight.' I felt as though I was travelling with a stranger. Who was this man who was offering to be my friend? We arrived at the house and were greeted by Mother. She was pregnant yet again! The pregnancy was to be a difficult one, for Mother was having the child, on change, as she put it. Well, at least she could relax after the birth of the child, knowing that it was to be her last pregnancy — poor Mother. Now that there were three grown lads in the home Father dared not rant and rave over the pregnancy. I settled down to civilian life in just a few days and then wrote a well-thought-out letter to Margaret. I expressed my feelings of confusion over religion. I told Margaret that I had discussed the issue with my parents and then decided that I could not allow religion to dominate any relationship that I had. I could not envisage myself having to live as the odd one out if we had a registry office wedding and then brought any children up as Catholics. I would be a stranger in my own home.

I thought very carefully before making my decision. I wrote a letter, 'Dearest Margaret, After much consideration I have decided that religion is far too dominant a factor . . .' I received a reply, 'My dearest Len, I understand . . .' The letter went on to mention Margaret's mother and *her* objections. It was all over between us, and for me our relationship became a life-long memory . . . a memory of the most beautiful, the most happy, and the most tender chapter of my whole life.

I began to visit my old haunts and continued my friendship with Ron. We played darts and we drank plenty of ale. I cried in my beer a couple of times when I thought of Margaret. More ale was a good anaesthetic and I drank plenty. The aching went from my heart as I began to settle into civilian life once again. I did not suffer for too long, for another female was to capture my affections.

Our new family home was situated near a golf course on the outskirts of Hull. The clean air of the industry-free estates made a pleasant change from the busy streets of old Hull. There were no belching fumes from exhausts and no smoking chimney stacks of industry. Clean electric heating had removed the need for chimney stacks on houses. There were no columns of smoke to be seen early each morning as people lit their living room fires. There were no shops available to the families who lived on the new estates. Mobile shops had to be waited for each day, and, if they missed, then families had to go without bread or milk or some other produce. It was not very long before people began to complain of the forgotten estates. No youth clubs, no shops, no play areas. There were no policemen on the beat and no police stations. The seeds of discontent and vandalism had been sown.

I looked from the window of our home during one weekend and saw two females. I opened the window and shouted. 'Are you looking for a couple of blokes?' My younger brother was in the house, and after the exchange of a few words we took the girls for a walk. I was about to have my broken heart mended. I began courting one of the girls for the next 18 months. The very first date that I had with 'Betty' (not her real name) was a most enlightening and delightful experience! Betty was to babysit for her sister and she asked me to spend the evening with her.

I could hardly believe what was happening as Betty undid my trousers after just a couple of kisses! We went to a spare bedroom and made love quite a few times. I was a very fit young man. Betty expressed her desire that we should see each other on a regular basis. I was not going to refuse that offer. We made love whenever and wherever we were able. We did not use anything to prevent pregnancy, I just practised being careful. I got a lot of practice over the following 18 months for Betty was quite possessive and wanted to see me every day. Although I was not aware of the fact that I had a drink problem, hindsight reveals that all the signs were there. I could not settle down in a picture house unless I knew that I would be leaving before the pubs were closed.

During the last years of the 1950s the leather trade was undergoing fierce competition from man-made fibres, and many small shoe repairers were going out of business. I was advised to look for some other form of employment by the manager of the leather wholesaler for whom I worked. I was not looking forward to the closure of the leather warehouse, for there was a very informal atmosphere at that place of employ and punctuality was forced upon me only when a visit from the proprietor was due. My activities with the sexually demanding Betty left me tired and exhausted, and I found it very difficult to rise from my bed. I was late for work almost every day, and I often took a morning off. Alcohol was also taking its toll as my system became poisoned with that fiery substance. I loved the stuff.

My younger brother Jimmy sold me an old Ford motor car for just £5. Lonnie Donegan had a hit record about a 'young man in a hot-rod car'. I fitted that description, for I drove like a man who was on a racing circuit. Betty introduced a new sexual experience into our relationship as she undid my flies as I drove along the road. We later stopped the car and indulged in some back seat sex. I shed another few ounces of weight. We made love in the car, we made love in the park.

The courting of Betty did not deter me from visiting public houses or the social club of which I was a member. I took the under-aged Betty with me and bought her a milk stout. We spent a lot of time in the pubs and clubs. I think that I only ever took Betty to one dance hall. She had often expressed the desire to visit a dance hall instead of a pub. I would always decline the offers that Betty made of teaching me to dance on the very rare occasions that I was persuaded to enter a dance hall. I much preferred propping up the bar. We began to argue quite frequently and I would tell her that we were finished. Tears and pleas to carry on our relationship made me feel quite guilty but I could not bring myself to conform to the nice-boy-next-door behaviour. I attended one dance because it had a late night bar. I had a photograph taken of Betty and myself. I was just a little bit shocked when I received the prints. My face looked drawn and haggard. My eyes were sunken and my cheeks were hollowed. My loss of weight was evident . . . weight that had been worked off by a very demanding young lady.

Betty started to question me about my intentions for the future, and made it plain that she expected to be married on her 18th birthday. I bought a secondhand ring for a few shillings just to keep her happy. It was a ring with glass stones. The talk of mariage seemed to dominate our conversation after that. I did not want the responsibility of marriage, but I wished to hang on to my sexual delights, albeit they were no longer as exciting as when we first began to indulge.

Familiarity is said to breed contempt. Perhaps Betty and I had become too familiar far too quickly. I would accuse Betty of looking at other men. I refused to agree to her attending a dance with her friends. I had to have my own way, the last word. I found it hard to accept when I finally killed off the love and affection that Betty had given me over that time we had been together. I had walked away from her many times and she had come running after me. I suppose I had it all coming to me when Betty finally took a stand against me: 'I am going dancing with my friend.' I said that if she wished she could go dancing every night from then on, for we were finished. I drove my old car home. I expected Betty to come to my home as she did so many times before after an argument. I waited for the knock on the door . . . it never came. One day, two days, three days . . . I went to Betty's home. Her younger brother said, 'She doesn't wish to see you again.' I felt numbed and I burst into tears. I suddenly realised that I felt that I could not imagine life without her. I begged her brother to ask her to see me.

She came into the house and our roles were reversed. I was the one who wept and pleaded, 'Don't leave me.' Betty gave me a fixed stare and said, 'I do not love you any more. You may as well go home, for I am going to enjoy myself.' I was given back my cheap glass and platinum and silver engagement ring. 'Can I have just one kiss?' I asked, hoping that a warm embrace might bring about a change of mind. 'If you wish,' said Betty. She stood with her arms by her side and did not respond as our lips met for the very last time. 'Is that really it, then?' I asked. 'Yes,' said Betty, and then she said, 'I'm going dancing tonight and I'm really going to enjoy myself. 'I went dancing last night and enjoyed myself for the first time in 18 months!' I was crushed. I was a very sad man. I drowned my sorrows with drink.

I visited my old pal Ron and we went for a drink together. I once again started to spend some time in his family home. His sisters had matured into nice looking young women during the time that I had spent in the army and in courting Betty. I liked the smile which his sister Maureen gave me. I asked Maureen if she would like to go to the pictures with me and her answer was 'Yes.' Her parents were not too keen on our arrangement for I was deemed to be a womaniser. I was nothing of the kind for I had always been a shy person. There were doubts about my intentions, and even my friend Ron asked me, 'Please speak truthfully. Are you genuine about courting my sister?' I was hurt by the insinuations that I was only interested in one thing. There were a few arguments about Maureen being kept out late. We only indulged in kissing, but I was treated as though I were some deflowering lecher.

Hostility over our relationship caused friction between the family and myself. I was saddened that we should be indulging in hostilities, for we had always been so friendly that I was considered almost one of the family. I was drinking large amounts of alcohol and was affected by it. I made a very rash statement during a heated argument that followed Maureen and myself staying in the front room until the early hours of the morning. I had never managed to persuade her into losing her virginity. I admired her for that, and I was probably reminded of the very chaste Margaret. My rash and bold statement was, 'I'm sick of all this arguing; we are going to get married,' and I looked at Maureen and said, 'Do you want to marry me?' Maureen did not say yes, she just opened her eyes wide in an expression of delight and nodded her head. I said. 'Right, then, put your coat on and let's go and stay at my home.'

We put the banns in and the wedding date was fixed for 24 December, 1960. We had been courting for just six months.

Chapter Seven

YEARS OF MARRIAGE

Neither myself nor Maureen had any money in savings when we put in the banns at the local registry office. The wait to the wedding date was not a long one and we had just six short weeks in which to find some place to live. Lady Luck smiled upon us.

I was told of a flat that was to come available for rent. I applied for tenancy and was asked when I would be wanting to move in. I replied that Maureen and I had to get some furniture together first. 'Ah,' said the lady who was an agent for the owner of the flat. 'I have a three-piece suite for sale, and I know someone who has a double bed.' Things were starting to look good for a young couple who were starting out with just their love for each other. Wedding presents provided quite a lot of the things that we would need. My parents were happy about the forthcoming marriage. My future in-laws did not approve, but Maureen and I were old enough to marry without consent and so they accepted the situation. My future mother-in-law said, 'I think you are both mad.' Hindsight tells me that we were very foolish to have married in such haste. A marriage cannot survive on love alone, and, regardless of what the idealists say, material things are very important.

I had just £5 in my pocket on the day that I wed. Maureen had very little more that that. I was absolutely legless when I arrived at the registry office, and my memories of the marriage service are very vague indeed. I do remember giving my mother-in-law a peck on the check after the ceremony. 'I still think you are both mad,' she said.

Because of the Christmas holiday period, Maureen and I were not able to organise ourselves immediately in our flat and so were catered for by Maureen's elder brother and his wife. We consummated our marriage in a borrowed bed. I was far too drunk to remember what I felt as I finally made love with Maureen. I do remember the next day. I thought it was fabulous. I took no precautions because we were married and did not have to. I had not thought about pregnancy.

Being married did not deter me from following my usual pursuits on a Saturday afternoon. I was working as a driver salesman for a local bleach firm and Saturday was the day when all the drivers went for a drink and a game of dominoes. I saw no reason to stop my Saturday afternoon social outing. Maureen was not too pleased about my Saturday afternoon with the chaps from work. I was not at all pleased about being told that I should stop visiting the pub now that I was married. I said, 'I have no intention of changing my Saturday routine — us lads always get together on a Saturday afternoon.' We had been married for about a week and here we were having our first argument. Another week passed and my poor wife started to suffer from morning sickness. My mother-in-law was at the flat when I arrived home from work one evening. 'Maureen is going to have a baby,' she said. The pregnancy was to be a difficult one. Blood pressure caused bleeding of the gums, and her sickness — which had started early — was to keep her awake at night.

It meant that she was unable to continue with her job as we had planned, and with only my wage to rely on things were to become very difficult. I was already in the grip of alcoholism, and so when poor Maureen was admitted to hospital because of her sickness I just 'pissed away' money which should have been put aside for rent and other commitments. I was drunk when I paid my visits to the hospital to see poor Maureen, who was unaware of the unpaid bills and rent. She was not happy in hospital and so signed herself out. Arguments followed as the poor woman discovered that we were owing rent.

Things were getting off to a very poor start indeed, and Maureen went back to her mother. There were some very heated arguments as I demanded that she return home, and I accused her mother of encouraging her to leave me. Both women had visited a legal adviser and been asked the question, 'Did he drink before you married him?' and when the answer was 'Yes' the legal man said, 'Well, you knew what to expect then.' Divorce was not an easy escape in those far-off days. Maureen told me of the statement that had been made to her after we had made up, and she added, 'You bloody men are all the same — you all stick together.'

The pregnancy progressed, and Maureen was taken into the maternity hospital. Our first daughter, Lynn, was born on 15 September 1961, just short of nine months after we had wed. I had a surge of energy and I decorated the flat. I expected Maureen to be pleased when she arrived home with the baby. One look at the recently decorated room, and the words, 'I don't like that wallpaper!' were enough to trigger me into a violent reaction, the first of many. I had worked through the night to have the room ready for her return and, because I am an incurable romantic, I had expected her to be very pleased. I had an image of a happy homecoming and kisses and affection. I had never been of a violent nature before that day, and later expressed surprise at myself. I ripped and tore the wallpaper, I upturned a small table and cursed and swore at my shocked wife. 'Perhaps you prefer it this way!' I shouted as I turned the place upside down.

Maureen had shattered that dream which I had nurtured. That happy scene when husband and wife have a loving relationship, free from arguments. A dream of rearing children in a happy and violence-free environment. Maureen was to find out that every time she started an argument I would become very angry indeed. 'Peace is all I want! . . peace and happiness!' I would shout. I would beg her to be happy. I asked, 'Why can't you just discuss an issue instead of creating a scene. I sometimes have to try and guess what is making you so awkward.'

Someone suggested that we argued because we were both born under the sign of Aries. I believe that we were just not compatible, and that if we had not been rushed into marriage our courtship would not have lasted — despite the fact that I had a great respect for the chastity that Maureen possessed.

I helped with the feeds for our daughter and I helped rinse out nappies in the back yard. Maureen was not to be outdone — she went back to her mother. 'Perhaps if she had another child it might stop her from running off every few days?' was the thought that went through my mind. Maureen became pregnant again and gave birth to twins just one year after the birth of daughter Lynn. I escaped from the flat at every opportunity. I found it far easier to go for a drink than I did to stay and argue. My in-laws put all the blame for our arguments upon me, though — to her credit — Maureen confessed to the fact that she was the cause of most of our arguments and said, 'I don't know why I do it . . . I just do.' She went on to say, 'You would be better off if you left me.' I had not gone into a marriage to fail, yet my increasing dependence upon drink was to increase the tension over the years that we stayed together. Maureen was constantly told by her family, 'You were warned about him.' I do not believe now that I had ever done anything really wrong that deserved my being blamed for our arguments — at that stage.

I became tired and depressed over the fact that my boyhood dream of a happy marriage was not materialising. I could not be bothered to put much effort into my job as a salesman and my work suffered. Angry shop keepers rang my firm to say that I had not called on them for weeks, and that they were out of stock of the bleach that our firm sold. I took days off after having had a restless night trying to sleep on the couch. I was called into the office by the manager. I was asked to take out two round books and complete them both in the one day so as to satisfy those customers who were out of stock. I refused to do two rounds on one day and so received one week's pay in lieu of notice . . . and my employment card. My wife started to say something after I had told her of my dismissal. 'Don't start now because I am not in the mood for an argument,' I said. I had liked my job and was very sad that I had lost it. My plea for silence was ignored and something snapped. I struck out at what I saw as the cause of my troubles. A blacked eye for my wife was the result of my striking out.

I was saddened by the behaviour that was preventing reasonable discussion of our differences. I was saddened by the lack of communication

. . . the running back to Mother. I no longer had any inclination towards being a good salesman. 'Screw the job' was my terse statement when I lay in bed one morning after my wife had given me a few nudges. I had promised to go and beg for another chance from my boss. I reflected upon the futile attempts to obtain a happy atmosphere at home, and I recalled those violent times of my childhood when Father caused so much despair. During arguments I would hate my wife. I wanted to silence her, and in my mind portrayed scenes of strangulation or of beating to a pulp those lips which were spewing out aggressive words. How do I stop this woman who makes me so angry? Smack! I hit her. Well, if ever she wanted an excuse to run back to Mother she now had a good one. I said, 'Every time you open your mouth to argue from now on I'll punch you in it.'

I enjoyed life as a salesman and obtained a job with a local bread and confectionery establishment. I liked the job because it was different. I met people who were friendly towards me, and I felt a sense of responsibility as I delivered 'three small meat pies before eleven a.m.' so that some housewife could have the pies warmed through for dinner at twelve noon. I sold other products such as sausages and packed bacon. The effect of the bickering by my wife was that I did not take too kindly to a hostile female voice. When I was late on my rounds because of a delay by the bakery department, some woman started to have a go at me. I just left my customers standing as I climbed into my van and drove back to the depot. 'I've finished,' I said and asked for my cards. I was asked to calm down and reconsider my decision. I allowed myself to be persuaded to resume the round with a supervisor accompanying me. There was more bickering by irate females and that was enough to make my quitting the job become definite. I agreed to work for the final two days of the working week in a different area.

I was selling bread in an area which had been a good residential area, but was now an area of bedsits. The bleach firm for whom I had worked sold cleansing fluids in bulk. As I served a customer I was spotted by the boss of the bleach firm who said to his driver (I was later told), 'Why is it that one of my best salesmen is driving a bread van?' The boss was told of my dispute with the new manager who had sacked me. I was approached by the boss who said, 'Take that van back where it came from and report for work with my firm in the morning.' I was delighted. Regardless of the protestations by the manager that I had not been doing my job thoroughly, the boss sacked him and re-instated me. I was so pleased, to be back with the firm that I moderated my drinking until I had finished my rounds. There were no further complaints from customers.

Despite the fact that I was feeling happy over my reprieve I did not carry that happiness into my home. I had been given a £1 per week rise but did not tell Maureen. Beer was still a cheap commodity for a toper and £1 bought about 15 pints. Sherry from the wood cost 3s a pint (15p) and cider about the same for a two-pint bottle. I did not start drinking the cheap sherry until around 1970/71. I very rarely found my wife at home after I returned from my work, and made countless trips to my mother-in-law's.

I tired of the almost daily routine of having to ask my wife to come home, and I tired of asking her if it would be too much to expect her to prepare a meal — just as other wives did in readiness for their husbands returning from work.

My boss was past retiring age and sold the business to another bleach firm. 'I'm not bothered who sells the most,' said the new boss. 'It is last in, first out.' I was one of the last in and I walked home that night feeling very sad as I wondered where next. I was given one week's notice. Jobs columns in the local newspaper were long. There were plenty of vacancies in many different fields and I could not settle in any of the many jobs that I tried after leaving the bleach firm. I just refused to get out of my bed when I had had enough of a particular job. I felt as though I had come to a dead-end. I had no motivation and no energy. There were no easy hand-outs from the Social Security offices, and, if a person refused to go for a job which the clerk at the unemployment office offered, then benefit was stopped. I was offered jobs labouring. My wife had to apply for National Assistance and was eventually given a small amount of money for herself and the children.

I filled in a form to say that we could not manage on the small amount of money given in benefit. There were most certainly no incentives for the idle to remain jobless. People were told to sell their possessions if they were not classed as necessities. A radio or a TV set was classed as luxury, as were pianos. Claimants had to hide goods when a visitor was due to call. Women were urged to get rid of their jobless husbands before they could make a separate claim if the husband was disqualified from receiving benefit. If a man picked up a cigarette end from the street and smoked it as he awaited his turn at the benefits office, he would be told, 'If you can afford to smoke you should not be here.' 'But I found it in the street!' would be the protest. 'They all say that,' replied the benefits officer. Frustrated men would attack those arrogant officers who were remnants of the old brigade of the Thirties and Forties.

I became increasingly angry against authority as I was forced to accept labouring jobs which were low paid unless overtime was worked. Even when I was put into a job that was too heavy for me and my boss gave me notice, there were three days' loss of benefits which were called waiting days. I did obtain a good job working in a warehouse. The money was good and the staff were friendly. There was overtime to be had and so I had plenty of drinking money. It never occurred to me that monies paid as overtime should be shared with my wife. I looked upon overtime money as something for which I had given my spare time. I believed at that time that I was being fair when I gave Maureen my full basic wage. My thinking (as I later found out) was that of the alcoholic who attempts to justify his actions. I earned as much in overtime as I gave Maureen for housekeeping. I was acting in a like manner to my father. I developed a taste for Taunton cider and so began to spend more time in the flat. Life became a little easier after we obtained our first TV set. I enjoyed watching some of the very good serials such as *Danger Man* and *The Fugitive*. Happy evenings beside the fire, supping a glass of cider and watching TV were all very nice. I helped with the feeding and changing of the children. There were some brief periods of time when my childhood dream of a happy and caring marriage seemed possible. Maureen shattered that dream as she gave me the silent treatment for no apparent reason.

'What is the reason for your going off into a mood?' I asked many times. I was often given the answer. 'Do I have to have a reason?' I would eventually become very angry. 'I'm going out,' I would say as I reached for my outdoor clothes. 'Ah, yes! You have been wanting to go out all evening. You only pretend to watch the TV!' The marriage was doomed from the beginning. I took a day off work after a heavy boozing session that had followed one of those irritating arguments. We began to fight and I was humiliated when my workmates would point to my scratches and pass such remarks as, 'She has you under the hammer alright!' The scratches on my face led to some very nice sympathy being given by a concerned female with whom I worked. 'I would be kind to you if you were my husband,' said the shapely woman. 'Why can't you be nice to me now?' I asked. We made love behind a large stack of cartons. We repeated our amorous episode just one more time. 'I'm frightened that my husband might find out,' said the woman, and then, 'I don't love you or anything silly, but I do feel sorry for you.' I had a few affairs during my stormy marriage, and it was one of those affairs which would end it. Divorce was to be the unhappy end of the shattered dream, but not before Maureen had suffered the harsh consequences of being married to a chronic alcoholic.

During 1963 I committed an offence — of theft. A cheque for a few pounds had been posted into my letter box by mistake. I cashed the cheque by going to a shop where I once delivered cleaning products. I was not given to criminal cunning. I was traced very quickly and appeared before the bench. I received a sentence of one year's probation. It is rather strange that my illegal actions were to prove beneficial. My probation officer asked the council to help with accommodation and we received the key to a three-bedroomed house. The probation officer was to prove that some folk who work as welfare officers have no idea of real life. I had quite a lot of hire purchase commitments and the probation officer said that the debts were a priority. I was asked to give almost a half of my unemployment benefit to my debt collectors.

It was very nice to have our own home at last and we should have become more compatible . . . not so! 'I can tell that you are itching to get back down the town to your drinking friends,' said Maureen. 'Oh, well, I must not prove you wrong,' said I, and left the house to see my drinking friends in the pub. We should have been so happy now that we had our own home. No shared toilets and no excessive charges on a so-called shared electricity bill. There was a nice large garden in which the children could play. Shops and a launderette were close by, and there was a regular bus service with a stop just yards from our home (but so was the nearest pub).

We had good neighbours, plenty of fresh air, and a fresh start, in a home of our own where we could visit the bathroom whenever we chose, and where only *our* bums touched the lavatory seat. (But our troubles continued.) Despite my dismay with our relationship I still had my dream of a happy marriage . . . a childhood dream that I wanted to come true.

I began to get involved in heated arguments and I also became involved in some very one-sided fights. I took some bad beatings from people who were much larger than me. I could not restrain my anger and hurled abuse at people over issues that would normally have been laughed away. I drank faster than any of my friends and so was told, 'You just buy your own — you're too fast for us.' As my tolerance of *all* people became almost non-existent I became an outcast. I was avoided by people in the pubs that I frequented. I found it difficult to get a game of dominoes as people said, 'I don't feel like a game just yet.' Yet minutes later they would be playing with other drinkers. I sensed that I was not wanted but did not realise that I was being avoided because of my attitude and behaviour which were both completely out of character compared with the younger me of just a few years before. I was already given to making statements that I could drink anyone under the table.

I did not attach blame to myself for the arguments and fights that I got into. I imagined that people were deliberately trying to provoke me. I am a sensitive person by nature and I felt very inferior and hurt when I was shunned. I would ask myself, 'What is wrong with me? Why do those people avoid me? Why do they find me so objectionable?' I imagined that people were talking about me. If some person laughed I thought that they were laughing at me — some secret joke perhaps? I would ask, 'What's the joke?' People had their happiness shattered by this madman who asked, 'Come on, then, share the joke — is it my chin? Is it the way that I walk? Come on, then — what is it?'

After yet another spell of unemployment I obtained a job as a milkman. I lasted just one day. I was then sent to the Corporation Cleansing Department about a job in the plant. 'We will have to put you on the bins for a couple of weeks,' said the man who interviewed me. I agreed to a spell on the bins providing that it was only temporary until I could take a job inside the plant. I reported to a driver as ordered. 'Meet me at Jesmond Gardens later this morning — about ten o'clock,' said the driver of the dust wagon. 'Where is Jesmond Gardens?' I asked. Hell, yer don't know yer way around yer own town,' said the driver in a sarcastic way. I have mentioned that my tolerance of people was low. 'Who the hell do you imagine you are

— bastard!' was my reaction. The man looked shocked as he said, 'Alright, alright, calm down,' and then he aggravated the situation by adding, 'Don't get your knickers in a twist.' That did it! I slammed my fist into the side of the wagon and I walked off the job. I returned to the depot and complained to the bosses. I was given a job sorting out glass and metals that were amongst the collected rubbish. The rubbish was tipped into a large cage that turned round and round so that dust was removed from the rubbish before it was to travel along a conveyor belt. My job was to stand near the belt and pick out the metals and glass. When the cage became congested I had the task of entering it with a fork and digging away the obstruction. I dug one day and was covered with chicken giblets as a huge plastic container burst. The belt led to a furnace, and many cats and dogs whose lives had been ended by a vet with a deadly needle came along the belt. Staring eyes that saw nothing, not even the flies that crawled over them. I tolerated those sad sights. I did not tolerate the belt for very long, though. I asked to be put back on the bins and was sent out with a gang. I was doing alright for a couple of days and then I mentioned that my shoulder was bruised from the heavy bins. One of the older men started to take the mickey. I made my way back to the depot and asked for my cards. I was told that I must work a week's notice.

I was given the job on the belt for a week. Maureen wrung her hands with despair, saying, 'Why can't you just ignore people?' I replied that I was not going to become a timid nobody. I hate authority and I hate pompous little pen-pushers who imagine themselves to be important and who — unfortunately — can cause havoc when placed in an unemployment office. I wanted to smash the faces of some of those people who made life so awkward as they refused to classify me as a salesman. I even asked to be classified as a driver: 'You are down here as a labourer.' I sought interviews from newspaper adverts. I smelled of drink when being interviewed. I had lost my confidence and needed the stimulus of drink. I needed drink, interview or no interview, I needed drink. I was drinking cheap sherry whenever I had enough money to purchase a pint or a half-pint. Without a drink on any given day I would become short of breath and my hands would shake. I felt frightened and my chest would feel as though icy water was trickling within. I had a dry mouth and feelings of light-headedness. My lips would feel as though they were trembling and I would put my hand to my mouth to steady them. My doctor treated me for nerves.

I sometimes had spells when I would have a surge of energy and enthusiasm. I smartened myself up from the stubble-chinned and scruffy drunkard. I applied for a job selling encyclopaedias and was taken on. I sold a set on my first outing for which I received £8. I was overjoyed that such good money (as it was then) could be earned for a few minutes' patter and one sale. I never sold another set! I plodded along on the knocker for over a week. I had to apply for unemployment benefit. There was more hardship for my wife and children as some twit said, 'You were self-employed — no benefit is payable.' My attempt to rejoin society as a working salesman was now costing my wife and children. I should have stayed on the unemployment register! I exploded. I shouted at the benefits clerk, 'How are my wife and children supposed to manage?' I was sent to the NAB. I was told that no payments could be made until a visitor had called at our home. Why, oh why, did I ever sign off and take the encyclopaedia job? I had to fill in many forms. I had to beg from relatives. I was eventually given a reduced rate of benefit. 'I have been punished for my efforts to earn money,' I said, and my hatred of authority and officialdom grew. I scanned the jobs columns in the local paper and eventually succeeded in obtaining a job as a warehouseman.

I was happy again. The wages were very good and I had the opportunity of plenty of overtime. I still gave my wife my basic wage and kept all the overtime money. I now had a very bad addiction to feed. I was happy at my place of work, but I was not happy at home. Constant arguments, lack of sexual relationship, and a constant suffering of the moods of my partner led me to spend many hours in the nearby pub. There were times when I would be pleasantly surprised when returning home to a wife who was in a good mood. Despite our constant arguments, there were times when I managed to make love with my wife. Our youngest child was born during 1964.

Maureen was finding it difficult to cope with the lifestyle that my alcoholism had bestowed upon her. I still insisted that I had a right to go for a drink after I had finished work. I was accused of not helping around the home. I said, 'I do my job *and* work overtime — what more do you want of me?' I had lost the willingness to help with the children. I no longer felt inclined to change nappies or make feeds so that Maureen could have a rest. I defended my right to go out for a drink. 'I work all day,' I said. 'So do I,' replied Maureen, 'looking after your bloody kids!' Only the wisdom of experience and hindsight can make me realise now just what the poor woman was going through. I felt as though I was being persecuted. I rebelled against all attempts to interfere with my drinking. I now know that all my reactions and actions were signs of the illness called alcoholism or a drink problem.

A few more arguments over my not helping around the home and I showed that irresponsible streak that is so common amongst all addicts. I handed in my notice at my place of work. I left that well-paid job that I had so enjoyed doing. More difficulties over money were to follow my rash and irresponsible action. I began to abuse the unemployment benefit by spending a large part of it on satiating my need for alcohol. Poor pregnant Maureen was at her wits' end. She had to beg from her mother and borrow money from neighbours. I was getting drunk and blaming Maureen for all my troubles. I staggered into the home during September, 1964. I asked the children, 'Where is your mother?' I was told, 'Mam is upstairs because she is poorly.' I climbed the stairs to find that poor woman was very near to giving birth to our youngest daughter. I ran to a phone and called the doctor. I thanked my lucky stars that the doctor came in time, as did the midwife.

I asked to be allowed to witness the birth. It was the most wonderful experience I have ever had. There is something magical in witnessing the birth of a child. I was very close to my daughter and spoiled her. She became a permanent baby to me. Even after she started school I would have her on my knee. I had feelings of panic, remorse and of fear prior to the arrival of the good doctor and midwife. I imagined complications that would be my fault for not having been at home earlier. I felt guilt. I was told by the doctor that he had been about to attend a function. 'You left it a bit late,' said the doctor. 'I should have been here earlier.' I said nothing. The midwife did not want me to be in the room when the baby was being born. The doctor had said, 'Let him stay.' Maureen said that she felt more relaxed with me in the room. With the new baby just a few weeks old, Christmas was approaching. She had been born on 8 December, 1964.

Many jobs and a few years later brought us to another Christmas. The children were all attending school. I bought a rabbit from the butcher after blowing most of my unemployment money yet again. A nearby church provided a few second-hand toys. I told the children that we were not like all those poor people who had to eat chickens — we were having rabbit! I feel sad as I recall the deprivation that my children went through as others enjoyed festive goodies, and yet I can laugh at those memories of rabbit for Christmas dinner and rabbit stew for Boxing Day.

During 1969 I obtained a job at Armstrong Patents Company making parts for shock absorbers. I was happy to be working a lathe. I liked engineering. I was paid as a setter/operator or 'top semi-skilled'. I took sherry to work in a medicine bottle. I could not see a day through unless I had a drink of alcohol — a good drink! My hands shook each morning as I awakened to the sound of my alarm clock and rose to make ready for work. I had saved 'a livener' in my sherry bottle.

Although I did not, and still do not, have much time for unions I was forced to join one in the closed shop at Armstrong's. I joined the TGWU and became a shop steward after putting my name forward when the existing shop steward retired. I was elected to represent the line on which I worked. If you can't beat 'em join 'em. Being a shop steward was a strange position for me, for my political leanings are towards the right. I was to earn good wages by putting in plenty of overtime — including weekends and holidays. Despite my fat wage packets, I found it increasingly difficult to satiate my craving for alcohol. My poor wife had to suffer as I opened pre-payment meters for more money. The gas and electric were eventually cut off after I had been charged with petty theft. Curtains were kept drawn and children had to have their natural playful instincts stifled as they were told, 'Shhh, there is a wicked man (the collector) at the door.' It is most definitely the innocents who suffer the most when addiction is present in a family (I welcome those groups that were formed for relatives of addicts) and *my* family suffered.

My body was being poisoned by the huge amounts of alcohol that were poured into it. I became tired and my body ached. I would suffer from pains in the chest, and my hatred of food caused me to suffer violent stomach pains as liquid ran through my empty intestine. I did not associate the lack of food with my constant visits to the toilet with diarrhoea. I said, 'I must have drunk a bad pint.' I began to suffer from sweating at night, and when I managed to get some sleep I would have nightmares. I had panic attacks as I lay in the darkness and I feared that to sleep would be to die. I felt afraid during the daytime if I was not able to obtain some sherry to drink. I began to fear being sent to prison if I appeared before the courts again. The money that I had taken from the meters had to be replaced. To the surprise of my boss I handed in my notice at work. I had decided I would obtain my holiday pay and my week-in-hand payment so that I could make good the meter deficit. My foreman offered me a good job on a new line that was to open at the plant. I had to decline the offer.

How sad was the hold that my addiction had over me, for, having left my excellent job and replaced the monies that I had 'borrowed', I became desperate for money again and 'borrowed' from the meters yet again. I had left my job for nothing. I was out of work once more and also out of favour with my wife. I appeared before the courts charged with petty theft and received a three months' prison sentence that was to be suspended for a year. I thought that I was lucky to have received a suspended sentence. I little knew that I would be called upon to do that three months! I remember feeling relieved that I was not to go to prison, and I promised myself that I would make an effort to get straightened out. I had received a lesser sentence than the one imposed upon my poor wife who had to face the neighbours after my name had appeared in the local newspaper. A new neighbour had moved into the avenue and I made his acquaintance in the nearby pub. I shall call the neighbour 'Ted'. Ted had a wife and two small children. As we became acquainted I learned that Ted had been in prison. I asked him what it was like. 'A doddle,' he said with a sneer of comtempt, and then, 'It was just like a holiday camp' (a perfect description as I was later to find out).'

I listened with juvenile-type awe as Ted told of his exploits in the field of shop-breaking. 'It's easy,' said Ted. I cannot explain why, but when Ted suggested that I accompany him to screw a lock-up shop I readily agreed. We committed the crime of breaking into the shop and we also committed a few more petty crimes, including stealing a car and stealing the contents of a till in a pub.

An argument with his wife led to the police being called to Ted's home. His wife said, 'I want him locking up.' The policeman said, 'We can't do that, love.' She said, 'You can when I tell you what he has been doing.' Ted and I appeared before the Recorder at Hull Quarter Sessions and we were both sent to prison. My term of imprisonment was 15 months plus my three months suspended sentence. 'Do you understand the sentence?' I was asked by some court official. Well, of course, I understood. I'm not stupid — I just act as though I were stupid.

Chapter Eight

A TASTE OF 'PORRIDGE'

How well I remember that feeling of disbelief that had come over me as the length of my sentence sank in. I had been led to believe that I would have received a total of about nine months. So said many ex-convicts.

My friend and partner-in-crime said, 'I thought I would have done longer than you — hard luck.' There was I then, awaiting January, 1971, when it was still January, 1970. I remember that I had a feeling that I had hit rock bottom. I was wrong, for I was to sink far lower. Divorce was only two years later than my release date. The truth of my situation after being sentenced to that first term of imprisonment sank in when Ted and I were handcuffed together as we boarded a police coach.

I thought of the words that had been used by the Recorder who had sentenced me. 'You have saved the court much time and trouble by pleading guilty, and it is because of that fact that I am going to be lenient with you.' I don't think that 18 months is a 'lenient' sentence for a petty thief who is going down for the first time. Thank goodness he had not decided to be severe.

I was not happy at the thought of sharing a cell with strangers. All my confidence had been destroyed by alcoholism. Lady Luck had decided to intervene favourably and I was placed in a cell with two young men who were not nut cases. Well, that was one of my fears taken care of. I had one more worry and that was violence. There was none. I had watched far too many films about prison, films that were not a true portrayal of prison life.

Before being taken to my cell I had to go through the reception area. Reception means being booked in and allocated a cell, being given a meal and being issued with clothing, taking a shower or sitting in six inches of water to take a bath. The cell in which I was to stay for a few weeks was on the 'Star' wing. 'Star' was the term used to denote a first-time prisoner. 'D' wing, third floor landing, and cell number ten — D3-10. My mouth was dry with apprehension when I first entered a prison cell. My luck was on the good side. One young man was a nervous wreck and the other man (there were three to a cell) was a little bit 'slow' but a pleasant enough chap. We all got on quite well together, but the first young man was a bloody nuisance. 'I don't think I can last this sentence out,' he would say as he paced the cell, using the very small passage of space between the beds. He would climb on a bed and look through the barred window of the cell, saying, 'I don't know how my wife is going to cope in that caravan without me.' He should have thought about that before he committed his burglaries — so said the other lad in the cell, and he added, 'If you can't do the time, then don't do the crime.'

The prison landings would echo the sound of keys jangling and of keys being turned in locks, doors slamming shut and doors that were being opened. 'Slop out!' was the sound that would carry along and through the vast emptiness which separated the two sides of a landing. Men with buckets would emerge from gloomy cells and make their way towards the small toilet area that had to serve far too many inmates. The stench of the urine that was poured into a drain would permeate the air. Buckets would be swilled but were cracked and discoloured. The stench of urine was trapped in those cracks and the stench would fill a cell as soon as a cooped-up prisoner passed urine.

There was to be no sleep for me during that first night that I spent in a prison cell. I lay awake reflecting on the past. I wondered how my poor wife would cope if some sly bastard attempted to chat her up now that she was alone. Would she have lots of hassle when making her claim for social security? My thoughts were interrupted by the restless young man. 'If I get a chance to escape I will be off like a shot,' he said. I did not feel as if I had slept that first night.

The cell door was opened by a man who held the keys to his brothers' freedom — a 'Screw'. Razor blades were issued so that we could scrape our faces. A shave was not a description that can be used when three men are sharing a jug of hot water and a small plastic bowl — there are no sinks in prison cells. Razor blades were taken away after breakfast and had to be marked so that the same blade was issued the following day. The blades had to last for a week. The facilities which are shared by three prisoners were designed for just one man. The very crowded cells are not exactly conforming to basic human rights. A man should have the right to some privacy if he needs to pass a motion during the night, and other prisoners should have the right to be free of the obnoxious stench that fills a cell when a man is taken short after the cell door has been banged to for the night.

I soon became familiar with such expressions as 'a shake down', which was a search of the cells. A 'dry bath' was a hand-search over the outside of a man's clothing. 'Snout' or 'burn' were the terms used for tobacco. Some of the prisoners would turn a dry bath into a laughable situation. 'Ooh what a lovely touch you have — do it again please,' was a bit of light-hearted humour that brought a solemn stare from the screw. There is a certain amount of resentment and humiliation attached to one's first 'dry bath'. I wondered if the screws ever felt embarrassed — perhaps they grew accustomed to it. I soon realised that such searches were only for the good,

and were necessary for the safety, of other prison inmates as well as officers
. . . weapons might have been carried. Another reason for searches was
contraband tobacco. Modern day searches are more likely to be made in the
search for drugs.

Meals were collected on large trays which had small wells stamped into
them. Carrying a laden tray up a flight of stairs was no easy task — soup in
one well and custard in another. Gravy slopping about in a third. Oh, what
the hell! It is all going down the same hole. Gravy mixed with custard does
not look too appetising. I practised a few times before I was able to climb the
stairs quickly without mixing the contents of my tin tray. Prisoners sit on
their beds when eating food. I have balanced many trays of food on my knee
as I attempted to cut a piece of tough meat, and I have had my plastic knife
slip and spill gravy many times. I spent much time either sitting or lying on
my bed.

Ennui is no stranger in a prison cell that allows no room for a man to walk.
I learned another phrase, 'Learn to sleep your bird away.' I tried sleeping
during the day. I lay awake all bloody night! I was told by some of the older
prisoners — 'lags' — that there used to be cell tasks that kept men occupied.
The do-gooders had put a stop to the tasks, saying that a man should be
allowed some free time. Oh! If only they had minded their own business! It
only takes a man a couple of days to exhaust his repertoire of crude jokes. I
was glad of the library books that were permitted.

Adjusting to a lack of sugar and salt in my diet was not an easy thing to
achieve. (I found such adjustment easy when I decided to give them up years
later.) I soon learned that those prisoners who did not take sugar could swap
their meagre ration — a spoonful — for a smoke of tobacco or perhaps a few
matches. I was pleased when I had stitched enough mailbags to earn a few
shillings and so be able to buy some sugar and tobacco. One of the other lads
bought salt and the third lad bought matches. We split our matches with a
needle — press the point of the needle into the wood and then split the
match. Some of the matches failed to split at the head, and other matches
were splitting nicely until reaching the head and shattering. The overall
result was that ninety per cent more lights became available.

As I settled into the routine and made the acquaintance of a few cons, the
stitching of the mailbags became much easier. I was shown how to make a
hessian thimble, and I was told that I should never undo the stitching on a
mailbag that had been failed by the workshop screw. 'Take it back and he'll
pass it,' I was told. The screw did pass those bags that he had previously
failed.

I could not help but laugh when I first saw a grown man having to raise
his hand and ask for permission to visit the toilet. A request to, 'Fall out —
stand up — boss,' was made when a prisoner was in need of passing urine,
and, 'Fall out — sit down — boss,' spoke for itself. Some of the prison
officers would deliberately ignore the requests to visit the toilet by

pretending to read a book. The occasional glance upwards would show the officer there were quite a lot of raised hands. He would look around the faces and if he did not like what he saw he would ignore some man in favour of another. One young screw was a bastard. He failed many bags each day, thus depriving men of a few pence towards tooth-paste or some other commodity, including letters. One letter was issued to a man each week and any more (we were allowed two more) had to be paid for. I remember how I started to unpick my first mailbag. 'What are you doing?' asked a seasoned convict. 'I've just counted these stitches and I've only got seven to the inch,' I said. 'We're not in the 1940s now, kid,' I was told. Some officers were alright, others were not. 'Nasty bastards,' was one of the more polite references that were made to prison officers. I found that most of the officers were sociable, even the ones who referred to our cells as kennels!

Sunday evenings in the prison brought some relief for men who were couped up in cells for most of the day. We were given a film show. The first film that I saw in the Leeds prison was a King Fu starring Bruce Lee. I was able to accept my sentence and so was not at all depressed. The same could not be said of the cell-pacing young burglar who should have occupied the lower bunk but who was too restless to do so. I buried my head in a book and so became oblivious to the poor young man whose bird was dragging.

Porridge, Stir, Bird, Pokey, Chalky. There were many different ways of describing a prison sentence and a confinement in the punishment block. There was some dispute about the reference to the punishment cell. Some men said 'chokey', meaning that men inside the block were feeling 'choked'. Other men said that the correct term should be 'chalky' because a bread and water diet turned a man's stool white — like chalk.

I read two very good books during the short time that I was in the Leeds prison. *All Quiet on the Western Front* and *The Ugly American*. After a few weeks at Leeds I was told that I would be moving to an open prison the following day. Hurrah. The cell-pacing young man was also going to the open prison which was at Thorpe Arch, now called Rudgates. True to his word, the young man escaped from the open prison.

The Thorpe Arch prison had those facilities that one could easily asociate with a holiday camp. Central heating, ITV in one room and BBC in another. Snooker, darts, dominoes, chess. I learned to play the latter after asking a thieving bank manager to teach me. Bank managers, insurance agents, labourers or skilled eye surgeons . . . I met them all in the nick. I compared the Thorpe Arch prison with the army. Prison was much easier.

There were no inspections and no rules about pressing clothing or polishing shoes. The food was excellent and a dining hall made a nice change from a cell that stank of urine. There were no bed-blocks to be made each morning, no order to swing arms as we walked around the camp — well, it certainly was *not* a prison. There is no deterrent value in an open prison, and so easy is the regime that most incoming prisoners are made up of men who were released only months previously. The Salvation Army hostel in which I later spent some time was a damned sight worse than a prison, and there is little wonder that quite a lot of inmates are old and homeless men who deliberately commit a petty theft as a means of gaining a roof over their heads, food in their bellies, and a few creature comforts. Some of those old men should have been in psychiatric hospitals. Others should have been helped but had incompetent social workers or probation officers.

I was given a job working in the stores alongside three other men, supervised by a civilian worker. Working in the stores proved to be very lucrative. A good shirt or a good pair of shoes could be exchanged for tobacco or some other goods. A prisoner working in the cookhouse could swap cheese or other food for different goods.

'There is honour amongst thieves.' Pish! Some prisoners would save up their tobacco and sell it for £1 per ounce. The rate or going price of tobacco varied with the season. Men who worked on the farms were paid one half-ounce of tobacco each day and the nick was flooded with snout. Winter-time meant that there was no glut of tobacco coming in, and so 'wide' prisoners who had hoarded tobacco were able to make a killing. There was plenty of money (still is, no doubt) floating around the nick. Men who worked in the reception were entrusted to stitch money into the civilian clothing of a 'baron' who was about to be released. How annoying it must have been for the released man who slit his jacket's lining only to discover some tightly rolled bits of the daily papers. Well, what could he do? I never heard of anyone going back to the nick to complain that he had been done out of a few quids. Another example of the lack of honour among thieves was the theft from bedside cabinets. If such thefts (of toothpaste, soap or sweets) were reported, a screw would pass the sarcastic comment that he was 'not surprised — this place is full of thieves'.

During the times that I spent in prison I never saw a fight between prisoners. There were a few arguments and threats but those threats were never carried out. Perhaps the thought of being sent back to a closed prison was a good deterrent at that time. There does not appear to be any deterrent now as stupid laws allow a prisoner to claim compensation if he is treated too harshly. I am one of those ex-prisoners who believe that a short sharp lesson is better than the holiday camp situation that does not deter. I cannot understand or tolerate those young men who have rioted in our open prisons and had the temerity to complain about not being able to watch more television. Send them back to closed prisons and birch them. What do people expect from a place which was designed for punishment?

The bank manager who taught me how to play chess had made some rather large and unauthorised withdrawals from his bank. Unlike most of the other professional prisoners, the bank worker (now retired) did not act in a snobbish and arrogant way when in the company of us who had been lesser employed on the outside. Crooked money men were given easy jobs in the officers' mess, the reception or the visiting room, or cleaning the hospital wing in which they slept. Oh, yes, segregation was in force. Those snooty, arrogant and despicable types slept in the hospital, away from us common crooks. A thief is a thief, and they were bloody thieves. Full stop. I took a great delight when listening to — and watching — one prison officer who took no notice of little rich boys. The officer told one man to stitch some buttons on a shirt. 'I do not know how to do such things,' said the foreign eye surgeon and thief. The officer said, 'Get that bloody needle moving now! If you can stitch a — eye then you can stitch on buttons!' The officer paused and then said, 'These lads do all sorts of things because they are prisoners and they are told to do them, and they do as they are told. You will do the same and you can start by counting these bloody socks!' The socks were those that awaited laundering and they stank. The officer had been quite correct. I was pleased that our civilian boss was on holiday for if he had been in charge of the stores the surgeon would have escaped his duties. Other jobs that I did during my terms of imprisonment were being a dogsbody to a civilian electrician, and making camouflage nets for the War Department. I enjoyed my time in the net shop.

It was during my time in the net shop that I witnessed authority at its most despicable. A blood collecting session was held and lots of men made donations. Those who gave blood were subjected to a deduction from their measly earnings for that short time that they were away donating!

An Australian chap was doing some time in the net shop and he stood next to me one day during a count. A screw said, 'Come on, you lot, get into line.' I put on my best Australian accent and said, 'Go to blue blazes.' The officer grabbed hold of the Aussie and said, 'You *what?*' but got no further as I spoke up and said, 'It was me boss.' The officer said, 'Let me hear you do it again then.' I did my (I think perfect) imitation of the Aussie. 'Hey, that's good, that is,' said the screw. And that was the end of the matter. I said in a quiet voice, 'Strewth, I thawd 'e was gowan ter do fer me.' The Aussie just laughed.

Sunday was always a day of decision, 'Shall I go to the church or shall I do some cleaning?' I chose to sit through the sermon. The churchman was very crafty — he showed a film from the Moody Institute of Science. I was fascinated by the wild life films, and sitting through a boring sermon was tolerated so that I could enjoy the film afterwards.

It was during my second term of imprisonment that I encountered that type of behaviour that is so common to, and belongs on, the picket lines that prevent democracy, that type of intimidation which prevents a free choice. The food at the open prison was first class. For some unknown reason a group of prisoners made visits to the dormitories at night and instructed the prisoners to refuse to eat the food in the canteen. A hunger strike was being organised. Those men who called for the strike were hard men. The following day the men left their breakfast untouched. We were all asked to sign our names declaring that we had been given food that we found objectionable. I am no hard case and I just followed the other men. Dinnertime was a different procedure from that of the morning. The sight of some big lads getting stuck into their food was enough to start everyone off. The unrest had not materialised. The troublesome men were sent back to closed prisons. There were to be riots in the prisons many years later. The trouble makers had obtained a foothold.

My second term of imprisonment was for nine months, and it was during that sentence that my long-suffering wife obtained a divorce. I did nothing to contest the divorce, for I was of the opinion that I should not stand in the way of my wife's route to peace and happiness, freedom from a life of worry. I was annoyed that my wife had chosen to kick me when I was down, but afterthought told me that she had been afraid to apply for a divorce with me on the loose. I knew that my wife had tired of hiding behind closed doors, and tired of scrimping for food and heating money. I knew that I was guilty of neglecting my responsibilities. My wife had tired of being threatened with eviction because of rent arrears, *my* arrears. I informed the prison aftercare officer of my having received a 'Dear John' and requested help in finding some accommodation to go to when I was released.

The after-care officer was yet another perfect example of incompetence — that type of incompetence which is so regularly exposed in national newspapers after the death of some battered child. I was assured that the after-care officer would see to my needs. I left the prison after completing my sentence and immediately became a homeless person. I turned to my mother for help. There was no hesitation. 'Welcome home, son,' said my mother as I arrived at her house back in Hull. My poor mother did not know what she was letting herself in for as she told me that I could stay with her until I found a bedsit. There were two younger brothers still with Mother and so I slept on a settee. I made no attempt to find a bedsit for I was far too busy drowning my sorrows and crying into my beer. Mother insisted that I speed up my efforts to find a flat or bedsit and, 'Pull yourself together, you are a bloody disgrace.' When I had enough money I drank myself into oblivion. I was shattered over the divorce. I secreted bottles of vodka after my mother insisted, 'I do not want to see drink in my house.'

I got myself drunk in Mother's home once too often and was told to go. I made my way to the Salvation Army hostel and asked for three days' bed and breakfast. I only had a few pounds. I was told, 'A full week's board or nothing.' It was nothing, then. I later spent some time in the Salvation Army hostel after being turned away but I never stayed for more than a week at a time. The craving for alcohol and a week of deprivation led to my getting hopelessly drunk before booking in. More drink meant that I no longer had enough for my board. I resented giving a large amount of my benefit to an organisation that threw us vagrants out during the daytime. I have been told that the rules have now changed and that men are permitted to stay in during the day.

I always have a place in my thoughts for those poor men who are still suffering the hard life, and I assure people many times, 'They do *not* choose the hard life.' Men who are mentally ill are even more likely to make up the numbers of those who live in the hostels, directly because of the closure of many psychiatric hospitals.

Shortly after that time when I had been turned away from the Salvation Army I obtained a bedsit. I had one of those brief spells of sanity that are common to the addict. I had, as usual, told myself that I must pull myself together, get a job, get a house to rent, find a nice woman to settle with. Dreams, dreams, dreams. I wanted a sober existence. I could not cope without the stimulus of alcohol and I was soon to be kicked out of my bedsit.

I lay on my bed. I felt afraid, I felt sick. I trembled. As the night began to fall I feared that death was about to claim me. I suddenly panicked as my breathing seemed to stop. I struggled from the bed in panic as my chest became ice cold and I imagined that my heart had stopped. I tried to swallow but my throat was too dry and I only made myself more frightened. A sudden intake of breath filled my lungs, expanded my tightened chest, and passed into my diaphragm. I felt a fullness in my stomach as the air filled that empty cavity. I had survived! My hands trembled and my lips felt as though they too were trembling. Lights flashed before my eyes. I became calm and took deep breaths. I suppose I had suffered some type of panic attack. I would suffer such attacks many times before sobriety was to bring me the return to normality. I would be absolutely sure that those attacks were the onset of death, and I was terrified.

There were times when I attempted to save a little money so that I could afford a livener from the little off-licence that sold sherry from eight o'clock in the morning. I was becoming worse as each week passed. A pint of sherry was having the same effect as what a pint of beer would have had upon me years before. Nine pints of bitter mixed with a couple of pints of sherry during a day, and another four or five pints of bitter and a pint of sherry during the evening. Sometimes a few sausage rolls and a meat pie thrown in. There is little wonder that, after a couple of wagers in the betting shop, I suffered hardship and poverty for five days each week. I could not ration myself after drawing my kipping-out money. I tried and failed a few times. I often wished that I was exceedingly rich so that I could always have plenty to drink.

The saving of a few shillings sometimes became possible if I had been lucky enough to back a winner in the betting shop. It was nice to wake from a drunken stupor and find that I had some money for a livener. I remember one occasion during a bad bout of the shakes. I had managed to stagger to the small off-licence shop to which I normally took my custom. I entered the shop and saw that there was only one customer before me. Whew! Not long to wait. The customer began to relate some gossip to the manageress of the shop. 'Stop yapping and get me served!' I shouted. My hands were shaking and my breathing was laboured. The woman behind the counter started to reprimand me. I interrupted with the words, 'I am sorry, I am sorry! *Please* get me some sherry.' 'Give me your bottle,' said the lady. She did not use a measure as she filled my bottle to the top (about 1¾ pints) and charged me the price of a pint: 'Why don't you do something about your drinking, Len? You are killing yourself — and you are becoming a very nasty person.' I repeated that I was very sorry and rushed from the shop, screwing off the cap from the bottle as I did so. I gulped down the amber coloured liquid and immediately felt better as the warmth spread through my stomach. I gulped another large mouthful. I opened the door of the off-licence and said, 'I really am sorry about being rude.' I was told not to do it again.

I hated life in a bedsit. I would wish I had a house of my own. My wish was to come true after I had been thrown out of my bedsit. I did not think the room worthy of a rent and considered that the landlord was some type of a rapacious Rachman. Exact times of year or dates are very vague, but I believe the year was 1975. Life in the bedsit had not been to my liking. I feared death more than anyone else and a small room would make me more fearful. I imagined that I would be found dead in a bedsit.

Having been evicted from that small room which I hated, I made a visit to my mother's. I was greeted with the words, 'I'm glad you've come. There is a small house vacant and I have just secured you the tenancy.' I was pleased that I now had a roof over my head and my own toilet and sink. The small terraced house was almost to become my funeral pyre. I did nothing to improve the décor, I did not pay my rent, and I failed to pay my electricity bills. I had much suffering ahead of me. I did not use the upstairs for I was 'frightened of the bogeymen'.

I lived, and slept fully clothed on an old settee in the kitchen. Candles cast flickering shadows on the walls. I had been given the chance to make good in a home of my own and I fluffed that chance. The house became littered with empty trays that had held ready dinners. Other trays held burned dinners that I had forgotten to take out of the oven (before my supply was disconnected). My house stank. I ceased to shave because I did not have any wish to conform. If I had been meant to have a smooth chin, then nature would have given me one. I spent much of my time in a graveyard speaking to the graves. 'You are out of this rat race. You do not have to suffer this world which is filled with bastards,' and 'Society stinks!' I shouted out my hatred of officialdom.

I would stagger back to my house and comment as I sat amid the empty tins and bottles and newspapers, 'Why should I bother to clean this place. No-one ever comes to see me.' I felt sorry for myself and wallowed in self-pity. I did not like being alone, and I missed my chair by the fire and my wife and children. remorse, self-pity, guilt and despair were all upon me as I declared, 'I do not care about living any longer — if I were to drop dead now I would not be bothered.' I spoke to the graves on many occasions and said such things as, 'If I did die in this cemetery she (my ex-wife) would be sorry and filled with guilt.' I have wondered if some suicides are attempts to punish others. I suppose some are.

A kindly neighbour who was aware that my fuel supply had been disconnected gave me a paraffin heater which needed to be cleaned. Mother had become very concerned for my health and well-being. She asked a psychiatrist to call and see me. I was not informed of the visit. I sat looking at my filthy home and decided, 'I'm going to get this place tidied up.' I set to and made a thorough job of cleaning the place. I then bought some razor blades and some soap and gave myself a 'spruce up'. I turned out a drawer and found a reasonably clean (albeit fusty) shirt to wear. There was a knock at my door and, upon answering it, I was confronted by a very important looking person. Well now, I had applied to the Social Security for help in getting my electricity supply restored. I assumed the man to be from that department. The man came into my home and looked around. 'You appear to keep this place tidy, and also yourself,' said the man. 'I try my best,' I said. The man asked me if I drank much alcohol. I did not see the point in his asking me that question, I thought we were going to discuss my electricity supply. I told the man that I drank occasionally but only small amounts. The man asked me some more questions and then left. Well, it turned out that the man was a psychiatrist and he went to my mother and said, 'There is nothing wrong with your son, My time has been wasted!' Famous last words.

Just two weeks after the wasted visit I was almost roasted alive. I attempted to clean my faulty paraffin heater by using petrol to dry the well that held the wick. Rust had settled in the well and I tried to blow that rust out with a cycle pump. The paraffin would not evaporate so I decided that a couple of tubes of petrol would help. The first tube was sprinkled on the flaked rust and lit. It dried out and I blew it clear — clever old me! I used the other tube of petrol to soak the remaining flakes of rust. I once more set light to the petrol and . . . Whoosh! A sheet of flame shot from the heater and burned the skin from my chin and forehead. Flames and smoke began to fill the room and I realised that there was only one way out. The heater was blocking that exit. I remember making the decision to grab the heater and move it so that I could escape, and I clearly remember taking hold of the blazing threat to my life and . . . blank. I have no recollection of my escape from the inferno that engulfed the house and destroyed it.

My mother tells me that I staggered into her home and said, 'The house is on fire.' I was taken to Hull Royal Infirmary and then tansferred to the a psychiatric hospital. Before being transferred from the Infirmary a nurse told me that I had called her a vampire as I ranted in a delirious way, and that I had attempted to escape by leaping from a window but was luckily restrained from doing so. I remember that the nurse had the most beautiful green eyes and a sense of humour! She would show her teeth and hiss like a vampire whenever she went past my bed. I also remember how weak I was, and how two nurses gave me a bath. Two beautiful women wearing sexy outfits were rubbing soap over my body and I just sat there. I soon became restless and eventually signed release papers so that I could leave. I was advised against it but my craving for a drink led me to ignore good advice. Just a few weeks later I was back in the Infirmary with alcohol poisoning. I am a very lucky man and owe my survival to the expert and dedicated care of the staff of doctors and nurses at the HRI.

I had no say in my next move for I cannot recall anything. I was moved again to a psychiatric hospital at Walkington (now closed). My first recollection of Broadgates is being involved in a game of chess and suddenly becoming aware of my surroundings. 'Where are we?' I asked my chess opponent, a lad named Fred. I was told by Fred that I was on the Ridings Ward. Fred beckoned to a passing charge nurse and said, 'He's joined the living.' I was asked to follow the charge nurse who led me into an office where I was questioned about the fire. 'Did you try to kill yourself?' was one question. 'I do not wish to die,' I replied. 'Why did you start the fire then?' 'It was an accident.' There was more questioning but I cannot recall what else was said. I had a room of my own and was pleasantly surprised one evening when a female opened the door and entered She asked, 'Do you want me to get in bed with you.' I made love to the woman — her name was Rose — and we sat and spoke for a while before the amorous woman left. I liked the life at that hospital. I attempted to speak with Rose the day after our passionate escapade. 'Go away or I'll call the nurse!' was her response.

I became aware that I was not in an ordinary hospital. My ignorance of psychiatric hospitals prompted me to think that I was in an asylum. I became worried and frightened. I sought the nurse in charge and asked, 'Why am I in this place? It is an asylum.' I was politely informed that I was in a hospital for the mentally ill, not an asylum. I liked the way that people sat very quietly, saying nothing. I enjoyed my all too brief sexual encounter, and I liked being clean and well fed. I liked having a clean bed and a bedside lamp. I was happy. I deemed the hospital to be so much better than a prison, and far far better than living alone.

I was pleased that I had a room to myself for I was a little bit frightened of the other patients. I imagined at that time that there might be some killers on the ward. Like lots of people I had a misconception of what a psychiatric hospital was like. There were lots of bruised eyes to be seen amongst the more ill of the psychiatric patients, although I must confess that I have never seen any of those patients hit each other — but then, I only saw those patients when they were away from their wards.

I was taken to the rehabilitation centre and shown several types of occupational therapy such as painting, woodwork, metal work and typing. There was a pottery class too. I was to learn how to type at the same time as I relieved my aggression via some verse. My attitude was deemed to be anti-social and I was given the label 'schizophrenic'. I wrote of springtime and birds one day, and of the occult the following day. Other days I wrote down my opinions of society. I was once asked the question, 'What is it about people that you do not like?' I replied in one word, 'Everything.' I later expanded my answer as I began to feel more at ease. I spoke of the attitude of the unemployment officers who refused to classify me correctly. I told of the despicable practice of the Social Security who urged my wife to divorce me so that benefits could be paid quickly and easily. I told of my dislike of people who orderd me to do things instead of asking politely. 'I hate people,' I said. 'Ah, yes' said the boffins. 'He most definitely is anti-social.' Perhaps every person who makes a genuine complaint should be deemed to be anti-social? Silly psychiatrists think so.

I do not like people who attempt to force their silly opinions upon me. 'I think you are an awkward person who wishes to be as much trouble as possible to others,' said one clever so-and-so. I began to feel as though I was trapped. I was being fed doses of vallium each day. I hated the attitude of some of the people who were in charge of patients. I was told that I was to move to a different ward. I no longer had a room to myself and was expected to sleep in a dormitory. I was frightened for the first two or three nights. Once I got to know the other patients I realised that they were non-violent and so began to sleep easy.

The ward had a charge nurse who was a friend of my older brother, Michael. I became friendly with the amiable fellow, Dave. Our association on the ward was to spread away from the hospital. But first I had some rough living to do — really rough!

The rehabilitation centre at the hospital held a dance each week. I enjoyed watching people dancing, but there was a nagging in my brain. You do not belong here, Len, were my thoughts. Elderly patients would rush into the ward and say such things as, 'We are going to the sea-side tomorrow,' and they would dance around just like excited children. How much better were those people than the people with whom I had been associating away from the hospital. I liked the happy expressions on the faces of the patients after they had been for a day out: 'We have been on a train!' and then, 'I wish you could have come with us, Len.' Yes, they were very nice and, oh, so innocent people. There was a treatment unit for alcoholics which was situated in the grounds of the Broadgates Hospital. I was to be grateful to that unit a few years hence, but first . . . yes, as I have already mentioned, I was to suffer.

I began to tire of typing poetry and took an interest in the pottery class. I began to make some very ambitious pieces of pottery. I made small animals and placed them on a rounded and flat base. I then made very small animals and trees so that I had a scene of cows and calves. The end results were alright and I later sold them to a ceramic shop for the price of a drink . . . nothing is too sacred to the addict. The pottery classes were attended by a lad named Dick who was an alcoholic. Dick and I became friendly and he listened to my story of ups and downs and of officialdom. I was told by Dick. 'You sound to me as though you have a drink problem and you blow things up out of proportion.' Dick asked me to attend a meeting with him. I lasted just a few minutes before I walked out of the meeting. I was not having patients questioning me! Group therapy gives each member the right to question another.

Despite my having refused to sit and be grilled by strangers, I had learned something that was to be very valuable to me in the future. I had learned that there was treatment for alcoholism, and I had learned from Dick the art of being honest with myself. Yes, I knew that my drinking was the cause of my problems, but I was not prepared to be parted from my beautiful amber fluid at that stage of my life. I stayed in the hospital for about a year before I began to yearn for the freedom of the outside. I began visiting a nearby town and got drunk on several occasions. I began to see the hospital as my home. I went out for a drink or a day in Hull visiting my brother and my mother. Going back to the hospital was just like going home. I suppose I had become institutionalised. Prisons, hospitals, army, regimented childhood and the institute of marriage . . . I had never been alone.

Life at the hospital became a monotonous routine once I had started to drink huge amounts of alcohol again. I became restless and argumentative. I wanted to leave and find a place of my own, but I could not tear myself away from the comfort and responsibility-free environment to which I had grown accustomed. I was in a trouble-free little world, free of the backbiting and back-stabbing of society. I got very drunk one evening and turned over a large room divider. The following day I was rebuked by a charge nurse whom I disliked intensely. I wanted to punch the male nurse but restrained myself from doing so — I hurled an ash tray through a window instead! I took a trip into Hull the following day and found myself yet another bedsit. I returned to the hospital and vented my feelings on the male nurse I disliked. I said, 'I'm leaving this place tomorrow.'

Chapter Nine

HOMELESS ADDICT

My life after leaving the hospital was not a happy one. I had grown accustomed to having things done for me, and fending for myself presented a problem. My problem was that I would enter a public house and intend to have a few drinks before doing some shopping for groceries. I would stay in the pub until closing time and completely forget about groceries as I ate a meat pie and drank a bottle of wine between 3 p.m. and evening opening time. The usual pattern was being followed. Sherry rather than food, and sherry rather than pay the rent. Sherry instead of paying a fuel bill. I had received a large amount of money after signing myself out of the hospital. That money was gone within days as I drank and gambled.

My family were angry at the reports of my behaviour in the days before I left the hospital. I was not welcomed into open arms as I visited my brother and my mother in their homes. My family were even more angry when I presented myself in a drunken state. I was eventually asked (or told) to stay away from their homes because I was an embarrassment and a bloody nuisance. I drank like the much-mentioned fish, and my food cupboard was bare. I sat in darkness when I had no money for the pre-payment meters in my bedsit. Rent arrears began to accumulate, and after having my final notice I was told to quit. I drew my weekly benefit and got drunk as usual. I returned to my bedsit and found that my landlord had changed the locks. I just shrugged my shoulders and walked away. I bought another bottle of sherry and sat drinking in a derelict house until evening opening time. My night in the pub removed the reality of my situation. I drank and I laughed.

I rejected all thoughts of the William Booth Hostel. I had had my fill of that place — and it was very expensive to a man who was in need of a daily supply of alcohol. There was a cold wind, and a few flakes of snow fell as I left the pub. Oh, well, too late for remorse now. I cursed my landlord for locking me out. I referred to Rachmanism yet again as I blamed anyone but myself. I armed myself with stones and empty bottles from the demolition sites and approached the flat from which I had been evicted. Crash! and 'Tinkle-tinkle,' as glass shattered and fell. 'Bastards!' I cried.

I hurled abuse at those people who opened doors or windows to see what was happening, and I shouted of 'Rachmanism' and 'Gestapo tactics'. My anger at society increased as I spoke of revenge against my 'persecutors'. I shivered as I staggered away from the scene of my vandalism. The cold snowflakes crunched beneath my feet as I walked around the derelict area looking for somewhere to sleep. I eventually found a house which had a small cupboard intact, and I managed to find a small armchair in which to sit as I awaited the break of dawn. The comforting effects of warm alcohol helped me to 'make it through the night'.

The first signs of dawn were heralded by the songs of the birds. I had not heard the birds rendering their dawn chorus since I did duty in the army. I heard the sounds of traffic and the whir of the electric-powered milk floats. I ventured out into the crisp morning air. I drank my last drop of alcohol from the bottle and immediately felt panic-stricken. It is difficult to explain the feeling that comes over the addict when a supply is exhausted. Fear, panic, desperation, despair . . . there are lots of words which could be used to try and describe the feeling. I pity those people who are still suffering from addiction, although I do not identify with those who take illegal drugs — they are usually aware that they are breaking the law, and they are well aware of the side-effects of their illegal activities.

I walked the streets until the public library opened. I had at least got a warm building to sit in as I contemplated my next move. I browsed through a few books until I had become warm. I did not want to leave the library but I had to do something about my predicament. When I had no drink my stomach would feel as though there was a wrestling match taking place inside it!

I began to have suspicions that people were watching me and condemning me. I had some crazy notions go through my mind. 'They all think that I am a hobo, but they do not realise that I might be a secret agent in disguise.' The world of fantasy was my way of easing the self-consciousness that I felt. I may quite well have been as mad as was suggested by a doctor at Hull Royal Infirmary. My madness helped me through some very difficult times as the winds of winter blew snow onto my sparse clothing, making it damp and cold on my body . . . bloody cold, and bloody damp!

As the early evening darkness cast its mantle I walked without thinking of a destination. I wandered more lonely than a well-mentioned cloud. People did not seem to exist and yet I was in the midst of people as I walked through the town centre of Hull. A train has a destination. The tramp who walked the streets in my clothing also had my identity, but he had no destination. As I managed to obtain a drink after meeting some old acquaintance who would give me a hand-out, I would once more be plagued by reality. I hated the sanity which invaded my mind and blamed me for the troubled times that I was undergoing. I fought a battle within as I lay the blame upon society and officialdom and sheer misfortune. I refused to admit my failings. Perhaps I believed myself. I may have thought that I had no failings. I really do not know all that went through my mind. I was very confused.

I recall those times when I would shout my anger to the skies and to the gravestones as I sat in a quiet cemetery. I believed that all my troubles were due to the actions of other people (I still maintain that some of them were) who made up officialdom, or Bumbledom as I preferred to call it. It was a fact that I was denied my correct job classification. I liberally sprinkled my rantings with 'If'. If it were not for arrogant clerks, I might have obtained a good job instead of being given a job, and if people had asked me to do things I might have stayed in some job that I had left after saying, 'Nobody tells me what to do — I do not like being ordered about!' It is, though, a fact that if I had been made a managing director I would have still fed my addiction.

Reality is far stronger than the drink, and I found it increasingly difficult to find that oblivion which would remove the reality that I hated. A reality which I did not wish to face. I had sanity enough left to know that my addiction was consuming me and killing me slowly. I really had chosen a very bad time to start kipping out. I lost count of the days as I shuffled along the streets. I wandered around that same area in which I had lived as a boy and a youth. The bulldozers had been at work in what was now a clearance area and all that remained of my boyhood home was a pile of rubble. I stood amid that rubble of dereliction and recalled days of a bygone age. A broken gas mantle with a large blue flame flickering through the hole in the flimsy material. The long chains that hung from either side of the apparatus and were attached to a lever that switched the supply on or off, or lowered the flame as people sought to make their gas supply last the night. A penny was not always available for the meter. I recalled the signs that followed a sudden lessening of the light as the gas supply ceased. Bits of old candle were hunted for in the darkness. The flickering flame of the candle made faces look like evil ghouls. A candle under the chin in a darkened room portrays an evil looking face. There would be a sigh from Mother and a resigned statement, 'Come on, kids, we may as well go to bed.'

Father had not been in the house most of those times when we were in need of a coin for the meter. I remember how he would come home late and drunk and put a coin in the slot. As I sat on a pile of rubble I remembered how I would be called from my bed to fetch fish and chips from the shop that the master had passed on his way home. Mother came to mind as I recalled the very canvas shillings that she cut for the meter. A tear ran down my cheek as my memories of violence came flooding back to me. 'Please — don't hit me in the face.' The sound of my dear mother begging for mercy from the vicious man who ruled us. All my memories seemed to come to life and I could hear the sound of furniture being upturned. I looked towards the spot where once had stood that dark little stairs cupboard in which I sat as a punishment. Despite my memories of violence I wiped the tears from my face and said aloud, 'I wish I was a boy again.'

I rose from the mound of bricks on which I had been sitting, and as I once more wiped my eyes with a dirty hand I made my way to the old Blundell's building in which I had spent so many happy hours playing with my friends. The sounds of laughing schoolboys and shrieking schoolgirls sounded in my ears as I remembered the games of hide and seek which were played in the huge complex. The empty buildings stood cold and desolate. Doors hung from their frames and empty warehouses conveyed the image of a ghost town as the wind blew small and dirty pieces of paper along the ground. I looked at an empty space that had once been a paint store and I pictured those men who had worn paint-splashed overalls. I imagined how those men must look after 30 years.

It did not seem 30 years since I had left the area to become a young conscript. There was no longer that little pile of plastic doll parts from which young girls had made such hideous looking dolls. There were no sounds of engineering from the small one-man firm run by a chap called Don Canty. Don was the brother of my very first employer. The two brothers had originally worked together at the newly formed Hull Gauge and Tool Company, but eventually they went their separate ways.

Another huge void marked the spot where many ice-cream carts had once been stored, and I felt my fingers touching one of those coins that I would seek in the sides of the carts. As I wandered around the old Victorian buildings I sought to find a suitable shelter from the elements, a shelter where I could spend each of the dark and cold nights that lay ahead of me. I found a suitable alcove but could not sleep. Perhaps I might be able to find a warmer niche. I wandered around until I found a rubble-covered flight of stairs. I reached an upper floor and found a huge pile of straw . . . now *that* straw would make a comfortable bed. I sank to the straw-covered floor as exhaustion overcame me and I fell into a deep and much needed sleep. Darkness was all around me when I awoke. I attempted to find the stairs that led to the ground floor but was unable to find them. I shouted from windowless frames. I was ignored by passers by — people do not bother with tramps. I was stranded. In desperation I struck a match and set fire to the straw upon which I had recently slept. I was rescued by the fire service who gave me a verbal lashing but did not prefer charges. Those people who had ignored my calls for help had fuelled my hatred of society. 'If I had been offering money those bastards would have soon got me out,' I said to a fireman.

Life as a vagrant is not a pleasant experience. I became far too dirty and unpleasant smelling for most landlords of pubs. I was barred from entering their premises. Aggression became my middle name. Over the counter payments were made to me by Social Security for I had no address. I was referred to as being NFA by the staff at the Social Security offices. Because I was obtaining sick notes from various doctors I was not being harassed by those silly idiots at the unemployment office. They would have sent me for a job interview even though I was homeless and incoherent. I was losing blood each day as I squatted over a piece of newspaper to empty my bowels of the watery fluid that filled them. I just gave up caring. I no longer cared who saw me as I sat in doorways drinking from a wine bottle. I sat on the public benches and swore at the passers-by. I fought with the other men who sat beside me. Plonkies always fight amongst themselves. I was just another plonkie to the passers-by. I had lost my identity. I spat regularly as I shared a bottle with my companions on the benches. We all spat regularly as a means of ridding ourselves of any germs that may have been on the bottle neck — germs from the slavering lips of those other plonkies with whom we shared.

Two characters who sat on the benches were called Hughie and George. I began to sit with them regularly. Hughie was a short fat little Scot. George was lean and tall. I could never understand Hughie as he mumbled away in a language that even his fellow Scots would have found difficult to understand! The only words I could ever understand were those that are so common to all who drink on the benches. When a passer-by was not being abused he or she was being asked, 'Spare a few coppers towards a bed for the night.' I shall always be grateful to George and Hughie (both now dead) for teaching me the art of survival. I was told of the convent which served food to vagrants, and of a school for Catholics where a cup of tea and a few biscuits were to be had. I had frequently gone very hungry before I met George and Hughie. George was a stereotype vagrant. He wore a long overcoat with deep pockets, shoes with holes in the soles, and he had large visible holes in the heels of his socks. His hair was flat to his head after he had taken a swill under a cold water tap at the convent. Stubble on his chin completed the image of the hobo.

George walked with a limp that caused him to lift one leg higher than the other. The short and corpulent Hughie walked with short shuffling steps and his feet very rarely left the ground. Needless to say, Hughie had holes in the soles of his shoes. Walking with Hughie and George meant that I became aware of more disgusted looks than usual from a few members of the public. I gave those snobbish people a verbal lashing. I can assure people that the aggression which is shown by vagrants is just a smoke-screen to hide their embarrassment. Of course, those people know that they are offensive to decency, and a bad example to younger people. Addicts do not like being the way they are. Addicts who have become vagrants are even more unhappy with their lot. There are feelings of inferiority and of shame and disgust. Feelings of despair and fear. Feelings have to be masked, and the vagrant uses foul language. Many vagrants cry at night when the critical eyes of a contemptuous public are gazing at a TV screen. I have heard many vagrants voice those same thoughts that went through my head. 'I wish I could turn back the clock,' so said many of those vagrants with whom I associated, and of whom I was one.

Tackling an addiction is one of those tasks which is most definitely easier said than done. Most addicts are terrified at the thought of being without their drug. Excuses for vagrancy and addiction are the same amongst addicts. 'I only drank heavily after my wife left me,' and, 'My landlord would not wait until I got some back payments through,' and, 'Our lass got my home.'

There are plenty of excuses to be had if the addict needs one. My sympathies lie with those men on the streets whether they be alcoholics or junkies or psychiatric cases. Very few of those men deserve to be there. There are some who pretend to be alcoholics when attempting to manipulate their way into a cosy hospital for treatment. The consequences of drinking a large amount of alcohol in preparation for a blood test have been fatal for some. Only a man who has gradually built up a huge tolerance can get away with drinking excessive amounts of alcohol. One man who tried to prove that he was an alcoholic so that he could gain admission to hospital choked on his vomit. He was aged about 30 when he died. There are more young people who die from alcohol poisoning than there are who die from drugs. There are many deaths each year that are associated with alcohol. I do not envisage myself ever going back down that road to vagrancy. Memories of vagrancy are strewn with memories of death. One young man started to visit the convent each morning. He was a real loner called Keith. The young man should have stuck with the crowd as the cold weather began to bring the snow and ice. He drank cold cider which lowered his temperature even more than alcohol normally does and died in a doorway in a main thoroughfare of Hull. He was just 28 years of age when he froze to death. As that poor young victim of addiction died in a cold and lonely doorway, his bottle had frozen to the ground beside him.

On yet another of those cold days of winter and vagrancy, I sat upon a small wall outside the very church to which Father had sent me as a boy. It seems that I was always in the vicinity of my boyhood home. Perhaps I was looking for something. As I sat wondering where I could escape from the elements I was approached by a chap named Tom who had attended the same school as me. He told me I was looking a bit rough and I replied that I was a bit rough and I was homeless. Tom said that his mother had died and that he now ran the house that catered for working men. Things were not quite as Tom had portrayed — I was offered a room at a reasonable price and thought that I was to be given a bedsit in a fully licensed (as it had been) boarding house. Tom's mother had rented the house, and, after the death of that lady, the tenancy was passed to Tom. There were rates and rent arrears owing and Tom was just sitting it out until the day when the bailiffs took control.

I was shown a room which contained a bed and a small wardrobe and a bedside table. I only ever slept in that bed once. Tom had not told me he was running a doss-house and that the bed was used at different times by other dossers, and a man who was having an affair with his friend's wife. I said to

Tom after a couple of days at the house, 'I thought I was renting the room.' I was told that I could 'kip in a chair, and if you don't like it then you can always go back to dossing out!' I was pleased to have a roof over my head during the winter and so began to sleep in the chair. I use the word 'sleep' lightly for I would only doze. I was not happy with the company that I sometimes had to keep as Tom allowed other alcoholics into the house, (Tom was also addicted) and I was often reminded of childhood as drunken men threatened violence.

My experiences after I moved into the open house that Tom ran are numerous. Tom appeared to have no sense of reality as he told me of a public house that had closed its doors for the last time prior to demolition. 'That contraceptive machine will have some cash inside it,' said Tom. I replied, 'That thing will have been emptied days ago, prior to the pub closing.' Tom replied that he was going to screw the machine and asked me to go with him as a look-out. Despite my brain being fuddled with problems I was able to see the funny side of the situation . . . 'Hull man breaks into empty pub and breaks open condom machine.' I began to laugh. 'What's amusing you?' queried Tom. I could not resist the urge to be humorous. 'I'm just happy about being a look-out man for a big time job!' Tom called me something nasty and then scrambled over the wall. A couple of minutes elapsed and Tom came back over the wall saying, 'Somebody's beaten me to it and taken the machine!'

One of the drunks had a reputation for carrying a concealed razor blade in the brim of his cap. I knew that the man did not do that so that he could have a shave with it! I consider myself to be very fortunate indeed that there are no slash marks on my face. I had returned to the house one day and smelled the lovely aroma of bacon bones being cooked. I looked in the kitchen and saw that the large stew pan was filled with simmering bones. I lifted one of those bones from the pan and ate the meat from it. A second bone was similarly stripped of meat. I then ate a plateful of the stew before leaving the house. I had completely forgotten about the stew when I returned and heard one of the men say, 'Here he comes, the bastard — I'll kill him.' I looked puzzled and asked what was the matter. 'You stole the meat from our stew!' I was told. It was at that moment that Tom entered the house and demanded to know what was the shouting all about. When Tom was told he said, 'I don't want him touched, or you will all be out!' Whew! Saved by the bell.

Tom had a talk with me one evening when we were alone. 'Why don't you find yourself a flat, Len, and leave this place before the bailiffs move in?' I could not bear the thought of a lonely bedsit again. 'I'll stay until we get the push,' I told him. The following evening had me wishing that I had heeded Tom's words, for as Tom and I sat talking there was a sudden crash of a door being burst open. Two plain clothes policemen entered the house and said to Tom, 'We've come about the stolen moped.' Tom professed his innocence of the theft of an old moped which I had seen in the yard of the house. One of the policemen said, 'Right, then, we'll discuss the matter at the station,' and he took hold of Tom by his arm. The other policeman took hold of me. I protested my innocence but was dragged by the scruff of my neck towards a waiting police van. Tom said, 'That lad does not know anything about the moped and is just a guest in my house (I liked the description when I later recalled the incident).' The policeman who held me said, 'Shut your mouth and get in the wagon.' Tom climbed into the wagon but I resisted as my anger grew, 'Get in there,' said the policeman who violently shoved me towards the van. There was a sickening crunch as my face hit the side of the van, breaking the bone above my right eye and causing blood to spurt from the gaping wound that was the result of that brutality. A detour had to be made so that my gaping wound could be stitched at Hull Royal Infirmary. I thought that the violent officer had acted like a pig! I knew very well that I would not have the remotest chance of filing a successful complaint. As a direct result of that police brutality I had the letters A.C.A.B. tatooed onto my fingers — All Coppers Are Bastards. I was to learn later that not all coppers are bad. The damage was already done at that time though, and I had my hatred of society fuelled.

More fuel for the fires of my hatred came as I sat upon a wall during a heat wave and removed my shoes. I wanted to let some air reach my sweating and sore feet. A police car pulled up to the kerb near to where I sat. I was beckoned to the car by the policeman who drove it. I asked what did he want. 'Just get in the car,' he said. I was puzzled but did as I was bade. I was taken to the cells and told that I was to be charged with being drunk and incapable. Having being stripped of my tie and my shoe laces and braces I was shoved into a cell. There is little wonder that my attitude towards authority and society is one of mistrust. I pleaded my innocence before the magistrates after spending the night in a police cell. I was fined £10. I was later to be labelled as 'anti-authority, anti-social and paranoid'. But I *had* been persecuted because of my illness. I had been wrongly arrested and sentenced to a term of imprisonment unless I paid for my freedom.

I became increasingly unhappy about my lifestyle. I wanted to escape from the company of other drunks. I wanted to get a grip of myself and escape from the addiction that I knew was the millstone around my neck. Tom said to me, 'The other lads have all booked into the ranch.' I did not pay much attention to what else Tom was saying for I suddenly started to feel very ill. I could not seem to fill my lungs with air, and my face began to go numb. I tried to speak but was unable to do so. My body began to curl up and my arms were drawn across my chest. Tom ran from the house and called for an ambulance. I remember most of what was happening and I was absolutely terrified and convinced that I was about to die. I was given oxygen by an ambulanceman. Two strong young men at Hull Royal Infirmary had a hard task holding me as I curled involuntarily into a ball.

My mouth was dry and I was unable to swallow. I was constantly being assured, 'You're going to be alright'. I had suffered some type of fit which I think must have been brought about by a mixture of anxiety and alcohol poisoning. I was later told that I had managed to remember the address of one of my younger brothers. My brother Jim told me a few years later that he had received a call from the Infirmary and been told, 'We have your brother here and he is quite mad!'

I had been told that I could go home. I walked back to what I saw as the cause of my fit — Tom's house. I have always feared drunkards because of the violence of my father. I still dislike drunken people. I have given up trying to discover why I became a drunkard. I just accept that I am an alcoholic who has successfully contained his addiction and can look forward to a future which stretches far beyond 'one day at a time'. I decided that I would take Tom's advice and get out of this rut. I did not find alternative accommodation in some bedsit or 'the ranch.' I found an empty building and moved into it. I was homeless once more.

Living rough was not a problem. I did not have any thought of self-respect as I sat with other alcoholics and drank in the streets. I wandered the streets cursing and swearing at passers-by. I was beaten by young thugs and left bleeding. Society does indeed stink. I ceased to attend the public slipper baths and I ceased to shave — razor blades cost money and I needed all my money for drink. I ceased to sit in public houses and counted my money in bottles of wine rather than in pounds and pence. I watched those people who went about their daily routines and I called those people ants and slaves to some rich bastard. I mumbled as I watched people rushing from one place to another. 'Look at them rushing to make some rich bastard even more rich. Look at them giving themselves ulcers as they worry for a rich boss.' I made remarks such as, 'See them all rushing back to their little boxes called home.'

My rantings were a way of covering up my true felings. I longed for the comfort of a home and a warm fire. I yearned for the company of decent and sober people. I no longer had a fighting spirit inside me and I was tired and depressed. My anti-social ramblings were now just an attempt to spur myself on as I felt the chill winds of winter penetrate my sparse clothing, chilling me to the bone.

I found an empty and derelict house in which to spend yet another lonely and sleepless night during which I would wish that I could escape from my predicament — but how? I had yet again gone to that area where I had lived as a boy. I sat in a windowless and cold house at the top of that very street in which I had played games of marbles or booled a hoop. The old house in which I sat had been used as a school for dancing run by an old lady named Miss Ridley. I called the old lady Mother Riley. There were no cupboards or larders with a door intact in the old house, and I tore old canvas from the floors as fuel for a fire. Despite my having kept a fire burning I shivered throughout the winter's night. In the very early hours of the morning I could take no more of the cold.

I felt the need to pass a motion and passed only blood from my swollen anus. I was hungry and cold and completely desperate for help. I threw an empty bottle through a small door window of a main road shop and awaited the arrival of the law. I was pleased that someone had taken me into a shelter even though the door was locked and barred. I received a sentence the following morning when I appeared before the magistrates: 'Fined £14 or seven days imprisonment.' I chose the prison sentence.

The screws in Leeds prison had a wicked sense of humour. They put me in a cell with a couple of chaps who were really doing some time. One chap was finishing a five-year stretch and the other was doing three years. The two chaps with whom I shared the cell were not as angry as the screw had hoped. I was the first to speak as I said. 'I know you two lads are doing some time — I'm only here for a few days.' The two chaps were not upset by the fact and blamed the screws. I was told that I could use the small transistor radio during the day when the two lads were away. The stitching of mailbags had ceased to be a prison task and I spent my sentence in the cell.

During the few days that led to my being in prison I had suffered a lot of itching around my waist and the insides of my thighs. I was covered with a rash which the prison doctor ignored. I later discovered that my rash and my irritation was being caused by the hundreds of lice that lay in every seam of my clothing. The lice were of the non-jumping variety. Such lice were known as cuckoo. A man who was infested with lice was referred to as being cuckooed. Because the prison doctor failed to identify the source of my rash, my clothing was not deloused. I dread to think of how many items of clothing were affected as my louse-ridden gear was stacked away with that of other prisoners.

My seven days in the prison passed without incident. I left the prison and returned to Hull and vagrancy. I did not continually walk the streets as I had previously done. I was tired of walking around the same area time and time again. I sat resting on the low wall of a church, and I had once again chosen to stay in the area of my childhood. The low wall on which I sat was one that stood in front of the small church which my father had insisted I attend so many years before. As I sat gazing into space I was approached by a lad who was a few years younger than myself. He had been a chum of my younger brothers and so I knew him quite well. I had drunk with him in pubs around the very area in which I sat as I was asked if I wanted a bedsit to rent. He said he knew I was homeless and he had seen me wandering the streets. He was friendly with Ken. I was about to obtain some rest from my aimless wandering.

I was happy in the bedsit that I rented. I was with friends, and the landlord was most definitely not a Rachman. I was to have a whole year in which to regain some of my lost energy. I do not recall anything outstanding about that year. I was content with my lot. We all drank too much alcohol.

As the months passed the time for demolition drew near. The other tenants had been in the house long enough to qualify for re-housing by the Corporation. I was about to become homeless again — unless I took immediate action. I visited the home of the woman with whom I had committed adultery before the break-up of my marriage.

I knocked on the door and waited for her to answer. There was an attempt to close the door on me as she said, 'I do not want you to come near me — you stole from me.' I knew that she was religious and so I played upon her so-called 'Christian charity'. I said that I had called to apologise for my past behaviour and wished for her forgiveness. I was then allowed into the flat. I told her of my difficulties and said, 'I shall just have to walk the streets or commit some offence so that I can go to prison.' My pre-meditated plan worked as she said, 'I could let you stay here for a while.' I put on a bit of an act as I praised her for her Christian charity and said, 'You really have turned the other cheek.' She was to have that other cheek well and truly slapped! I told her that I had only just at that moment realised how lovely she was, how nice her blue eyes were, and how I wished that we could be together for always. All went to plan and I collected my few articles of clothing and moved in with the gullible lady.

I suffered because of the moodiness of my unstable partner. I was asked to leave many times and I was also thrown into the cells of a nearby police station after that silly woman made silly complaints. The policemen at the station pleaded with me to leave the woman. She asked me one day, 'Where is your birth certificate?' I said that all my papers had been destroyed in a fire. I was asked for the date of my birth a few times. I thought that she was contemplating a birthday present. She had obtained a duplicate birth certificate and used it when putting in the mariage banns. I had always thought that it takes two, but she managed to arrange a marriage single-handed. I was told to close my eyes and then open them, and, lo and behold, I saw upon the hand of the maiden a wedding ring, and I was fraught with worry. The time had arrived when I must go. She misplaced her wedding ring as she toured the block of flats showing it to all her friends and neighbours. I booked in at the William Booth Hostel.

I was not to stay in 'the ranch' for very long. My addiction did not permit me to go for very long without a copious intake of the amber fluids that sustained me. I was only able to buy small amounts if I had a full week's board to pay to the 'Sally Anne'. I listened to the arguments and watched some of the fights between the men in the hostel. I looked at the blood-spattered stone steps that led up to the small wooden cubicles. I made a search of the old and derelict buildings the next day and, having found a suitable 'kipper', I left the ranch and its blood spattered walls and stairs. As I took to the road once more I was unaware that it was to be for the last time.

Chapter Ten

THE BEGINNING OF THE END

I began to blame the area in which I lived as the cause of my problems, and I also placed blame upon other people. I was not prepared to admit that it was I who was the only problem!

I was the one who did the drinking, the abusing of friendships and family relations. I was the addict. I was the cause of my many problems. I thought that if I got away from Hull I would be free of those problems. I did not realise that, wherever I went, so did the problem. I began to hitch lifts around the country with long-distance lorry drivers. I did a bit of loading and un-loading. The drivers rewarded me with a meal and a few pints of beer during the day and the price of a pint of sherry when we arrived back in Hull. The sherry was my comfort for the night providing that I could restrain myself from drinking the lot in a few mouthfuls. I would like the feeling of a bottle of sherry in my pocket to that of a person who enters a nice comfortable home after walking through the snowfalls of a cold winter's night. It really was comforting.

I would often tell myself that if I could stop drinking for a couple of weeks I would have enough for a deposit of two weeks in advance rent payments on a bedsit. I could not even go one day without a drink if I had money in my pocket, and so never saved a deposit. A few drinks, and I would just start my 'Rachman' talk again. I hated the nights of dereliction. I would now liken my feelings to that of a man who was lost in space. Absolute loneliness. Depression brought tears that became cold before they ran down my cheeks, and as I sucked at the mouth of an empty bottle I felt even more depressed. I would try to get my tongue inside the bottle to lick the last dregs of the cheap sherry, and I even tried sniffing the fumes from the bottle.

Some nights I was lucky enough to fall into an exhausted sleep and so have a 'livener' left from an almost empty bottle. I did not fall asleep very often and so suffered very frequently. I walked the streets when I was not inebriated, for to stop walking would result in my whole body starting to shake, and the fear of death to come over me. I was to suffer that fear of death for quite some time after I had stopped drinking. I became very jumpy with nerves as my body finally began to buckle beneath the pressures to which it had been subjected for so many years. Lack of sleep, lack of proper diet and endless walking of the streets were finally taking their toll. I suffered from swollen and bleeding haemorrhoids. I suppose that it would be quite true to say that I was nearing death. I hardly ate any food. Fate was preparing to 'deal me a better hand' as I trudged through the snow-covered streets of Hull. My eyelids were trying to close and give me some much needed sleep during the hours of darkness, but weird faces and huge spiders seemed to appear from the darkness and come towards me. Walking and walking some more. Stomach heaving in convulsions, ribs aching as I sucked air into my seemingly unfillable lungs, floating lights before my eyes. 1979 began to pass without my being aware of what month was on the calendar. I was only interested in the day. Was it benefit day? The most devastating answer I ever received to the question, 'What day is this?' was when a chap replied that it was a Wednesday. My whole body sagged with despair — I had only been paid the previous day!

I suffered such torment quite a few times, and I think that I must have gambled away some of my cash as I strove to get enough money for advance rent. I surely could not have consumed 23 quids' worth of booze in one day — could I? I had no timetable, I just existed from day to day. I visited the convent on Beverley Road to obtain food and drink each morning. I always felt at ease there for I was with people of my own kind, people who were homeless, penniless and friendly. I was able to have a conversation with fellow human beings. I cannot write about the convent without feeling very sad for those poor souls who still shuffle their way to that sanctuary from starvation. I get angry (as I did during my vagrancy) to see men entering the convent for free food when I know that those men have a nice warm bedsit which is being paid for by the DHSS. Fuel bills and rents can now be deducted from benefits and so there is no need for people to lose their homes as I did. The official time for charity from the convent was around 8 a.m. each day, but I was given a cup of tea when I arrived very early. I sat on the long wooden bench that was provided and awaited 'feeding time'. Other vagrants began to arrive as I strove to get breath into my lungs.

The familiar figures of George and Hughie appeared and I was a bit more relaxed. George and Hughie were both still 'kipping out' somewhere and I was to become eternally grateful that those two characters were still visiting the convent. As the kindly nuns spooned out a mixture of potato and cabbage with strands of meat I held forth my piece of old newspaper which acted as a plate. We ate with our fingers. Soup was available in plastic mugs, and, after giving the mugs a rinse, we then filled them with tea from a large urn. The Sisters of Mercy did not require us vagrants to sing hymns in exchange for our meals. The Salvation Army had a 'hymns first' policy before giving away bowls of soup on a Sunday. The nuns were very good to us vagrants and treated us as though we were paying guests.

I vomited shortly after leaving the convent each morning, and I would suffer severe pain in my stomach. Alcohol relieved the pain and helped me to 'keep down' my food. As each of those final weeks of 1979 passed by I drew ever closer to the end of a long and painful addiction. I was in my final year of that living hell which is called 'chronic alcoholism'. That final year was to be my most depressing of all. I felt helpless, and I no more spoke of not wishing to be a part of society, and, indeed, I wished that I could be a part of that society and enjoy the comfort of a warm home and a full stomach. I pictured a glowing fire and a full food cupboard. I thought of those 'money-grabbing bastards' who rented out the homes and I wished that I was giving money to them each week. I wished that I had a month's rent money in my pocket. I wanted to make the effort to accumulate enough cash to secure a roof over my head but my addiction was far stronger than my desire for comfort and security.

I spent much time in the graveyard as I sought absolute quiet away from the noisy traffic at which I hurled abuse. Even the tinkle of a cycle's bell would make me shout the words, 'Noisy bastard!' My nerves were so frayed that I would jump at the slightest noise. Even a sudden cough would startle me as much as if some motorist had sounded his horn. I was irritable when I had to queue to cash my benefit cheque. 'Hurry up, hurry up,' I would say loudly. I received some nasty looks but no comments. I must have looked very aggressive.

I ran to the off-licence and bought a bottle of sherry. I was gasping for air as my tensed muscles restricted my breathing. My stomach muscles would be tensed and my mouth was very dry. All of those symptoms would gradually ease as I drank the warming and comforting fluid. I would need to drink the whole bottle of sherry before I became fully relaxed. I would purchase a second bottle just for the comfortable feeling that it gave me to know that it was there. A visit to the local slipper baths gave me a chance to wash my underpants, socks and vests after I had washed my stinking body. I would just wash the collar of my shirt.

I told myself each week that I should look for accommodation after I left the baths. Each week I decided to enter the pub 'just for a pint or two'. I always stayed until closing time and said to myself, 'I'll hunt for a flat tomorrow.' After a clean-up at the baths I was once mistaken for a demolition worker because of my tattered and dirty clothing. My aggressive and insulting behaviour got me barred from some pubs, and my sitting for too long without buying got me barred from others. I liked the sanctuary of a nice quiet pub where I could usually sit alone all during the midday opening hours. I was once asked the question, 'Are you working around here?' I replied quite truthfully when I said, 'I'm doing my thing around the demolition area.' Despite my wretched existence I was still able to find my sense of humour.

Closing time at the pub would have me cringing as I thought of going out into the cold. Icy winds blew lightly-falling snow onto my already damp clothing as I made my way to the public library where I could sit until the late afternoon. I would try to read a book so that I could forget about the long and cold night that lay ahead of me — the aimless wandering as I tried to 'walk off' a panic attack. I heaved many a sigh of despair as I longed to be able to escape the clutches of my addiction. I was glad to have the price of a pint so that I could enter a nice warm pub. It was not easy to escape the eye of a landlord when sitting without ordering another pint of ale. I was called a non-consumer by one landlord. 'Are you going to order another beer or sit admiring the décor?' another one asked. Regardless of the hour that I left a pub, I could not escape the stark reality of homelessness as I shivered, looked left and right, and did not know which way to turn. I longed for the dawn of the next day to arrive as I thought of the deathly quiet of the small hours. Tears of despair ran cold down hollowed cheeks, tears of despair that were mingled with tears of remorse. I was aware that my actions had contributed to my predicament. I did not long for death or the peace that I imagined it would bring, but I did shout towards the heavens. I defied the invisible God to strike me down and 'Get it over with'. I was not to be granted my wish for an end to my suffering, and so I soldiered on.

During the last few months of dereliction I was to meet with quite a few different characters. I met most of those men at the convent. There was 'Little Len' who washed his hands and face but seemed to forget that he had a neck and two wrists. Three tide marks made Les quite distinguishable. I was later to meet up with him in a hospital.

Memories of events are very limited, for a brain that is being pickled in alcohol registers very little. I do not know how I came to have a crack in the base of my skull, and I do not remember the beating which resulted in my nose being broken for the third time. I had my nose re-set after that one. I often woke from a fitful sleep and realised that I had taken a beating. My eye would be blacked and swollen and my lips cut and swollen too. I can recall taking broken pot from my mouth as my false teeth were smashed by a blow from a fist or a boot, but I have no memory of the affray that resulted in the breaking of those teeth. I decided that there is safety in numbers and so teamed up with George and Hughie once more. I was pleased to have company for I had become afraid of being alone at night after taking beatings from young thugs.

We three vagrants would tuck newspapers into our clothing as we sought to keep out the cold. George told me which door to knock on for a handout from a priest. I was given ten pence. I was not in the habbit of begging. Hughie said to me, 'If you are not going to pan-handle (beg) then you'll get no bloody booze from me!' Hughie pushed me as he spoke. I launched a vicious retaliation. People who had known me before my decline into dereliction would not have recognised the snarling animal who attacked in self-defence. I punched and I kicked and I spat. There was little wonder that the aggressive Hughie reeled back in shock as I attacked. We pooled the few coppers from our pockets and George said, 'We have enough for some surge (surgical spirit).' I had never drank anything other than licensed spirits and was a little afraid of the substance which I was being offered by my companions. The surgical spirit was mixed with water and looked like a disinfectant as it turned white. It even smelled like disinfectant! I started to shake as I decided that I did not wish to drink that vile substance, yet craved for alcohol. I shook like I had never shaken before and George said, 'Hey, come on, kid, sup some of this or you're going to have a real bad time, you're on the verge of a fit.' I was frightened of the substance and I said so to George. I asked for the bottle of surge and took a drink. It tasted as vile as it stank. I drank some more and my breathing came a bit easier. George said to me, 'You can have one more mouthful and then you are on your own — the rest is for me and Hughie.' I raised the bottle to my lips once more. It was to be the last time that I was to allow my addiction to rule my actions. It was the last time that I would succumb to my craving for alcohol.

I had no money. I had no home. I had no idea of what happened to me during the final days of 1979. I missed eating on Xmas Day for I did not think that the convent would be serving food on that day. Boxing Day was a little different from all those other days that I had seen at the convent. Sister Theresa gave me a small glass of sherry as she said, 'You do not look at all well.' The kindly lady gave me a scarf to put around my neck and said, 'That should help keep you warm — and where were you yesterday?' I replied that I did not think the convent opened on a Christmas Day. Sister Theresa said, 'We never close our doors — never.' I was just a few days from seeking help. I cannot recall seeking the help that I so badly needed.

Christmas 1979 had been and gone, as had the eve of the new year. January, 1980, had arrived, and for this long-suffering alcoholic it was all over. A new year lay ahead. A new year which was to bring a new beginning and a whole new outlook on life.

Chapter Eleven

UPHILL STRUGGLE

I cannot recall the events which led to my being helped by my family once more. Those 'final chances' that I had abused were forgotten as I once again begged for help. I later had the story told to me. During the first few days of January (nobody knows the exact day) I knocked on the door of my brother's home and asked to be helped yet again. Michael told me that I was very distressed. I showed Michael my legs and ankles which were very swollen. I sobbed repeatedly the words. 'I've had enough, I've had enough,' and, 'I think that I am dying.' I do not believe in the theory that events are mapped out for us from birth, but it was really just a coincidence that the charge nurse of the ward that I had been on at Broadgates Hospital had opened a house that had been convereted into bedsits? Was it just coincidence that the nurse was a very good friend of my brother Michael? And was it just coincidence that Brian (the nurse and friend) had an empty attic bedsit? I could not have wished for a better set of circumstances as I began my arduous journey along the road to sobriety, a road that would end with a door to reality, a door marked 'Society'.

My mother agreed that I could stay at her home until the bedsit was prepared. Mother and Michael advanced me the money for items such as beding, pots and pans, and a second-hand television. As I climbed the stairs that led to my bedsit Michael said. 'Look, at the number on your door.' I looked at the bold blue number. It was number seven. Michael said, 'That must be a good omen.' I did not sleep that first night for I was wracked with pains and aches. I suffered feelings of anxiety. Going into sobriety is like going into an operating theatre. Frightening!

The following day I was taken to Broadgates Hospital and into the alcoholic unit. I had made the request to be taken to the unit because, 'I knew that I would succeed there.' Brian knew the nurses in the unit, and both he and my brother Michael pleaded a good case. I was accepted as a day patient only. 'We are not having him in!' were the words used by the nurse in charge. I remember being told by a senior nurse that I really ought to be attending the De La Pole hospital because Broadgates had not had any effect upon me previously. 'Well, I did not want to stop drinking before,' I said, and hoped that I looked sincere. The senior nurse went back into the office and I was left to 'sweat it out' before being given the good news that I could attend as a day patient. I was later told by the head of the unit, 'We didn't want you. We had seen enough of you to decide that you were beyond help.'

There is no doubt in my mind that if I had been taken as an in-patient then I would not have had the same type of success that I have had as a day-patient. In-patients do not have to face up to the responsibilities of everyday life. The hospital shields the in-patient from reality, and release puts the patients back into the same situation from which they had sought to escape. The day patient starts his battle from day one, mixing therapy with the task of facing reality away from the hospital. Once I knew that the hospital had decided to accept me as a patient, I heaved a great sigh of relief. I also shed tears of relief in the privacy of my bedsit numbered seven.

The battle for sobriety was not to be an easy one. As the anaesthetic of alcohol wore off I began to suffer the pains of deprivation, as well as the aches and pains that racked my battered body. Sleepless nights brought with them the thoughts of guilt over a broken marriage. Guilt and remorse and shame — there was no place for such feelings in a recovery programme that had only just begun, and I had no intentions of losing the battle. There would be time for regrets when I became stronger and able to accept guilt.

Travelling to the hospital each day gave me an instant routine which was beneficial to my treatment. I had to prepare myself each day by washing and shaving, and those two tasks were alien to me. Because the hospital was in Walkington I had buses to catch each day. Such simple and everyday tasks were not easy to adapt to for one who had alienated himself from society. I was given my fares each day for it was agreed that a condition of my being helped was that I allowed Brian to run my finances. It was considered dangerous for me to have cash in my pocket. I had to gain independence by results. I had to gain respect, trust, and credibility. My past actions had reflected only untrustworthy characteristics. It was almost two years after I had entered into a treatment situation, that I finally obtained my independence. I ranted and raved inwardly and in private. Gratitude prevented me from forcing my controllers to give me my independence. The waiting was a good test of the amount of tolerance that I was building. Tolerance is a very essential part of a recovery programme.

Having attended two group meetings each day I soon began to think in a positive manner. I could never remember all that had been said in the meetings, but I did learn that I was my problem. I was not able to relax for quite some months after treatment had begun, for my mind was a hive of activity. I just could not 'switch off'. I recalled hitting my wife as some other man in a group admitted to similar actions. Mothers confessed to the meetings of having been too severe with their children when not having drink available. There was a general pattern of behaviour amongst both the male and the female addicts. Total chaos and family disunity were common to most of the people who made up a group. It was a good start for any patient when he or she became aware of the fact that they were 'not the only one'. I felt a sense of relief when I heard others confess to having acted in some of those same nasty ways as I had acted when under the influence of alcohol. I was able to identify with those people who spoke of feelings of inferiority, and of unknown fear.

I was happy that I was a part of the unit. I was being 'understood' at last! My frustrations were the same frustrations that others were feeling. I was not alone. I found the groups to be very beneficial and very educational as others spoke. I dreaded being asked to speak in the group meetings. I was later told by a charge nurse that it was very difficult to shut me up once I had started to talk. The nurse said, 'It is harder to stop you from talking — much harder than it was to ever get you started!' I took that as a progress report. My one positive statement regarding group therapy is, 'It worked for me.'

It is said that 'Confession is good for the soul' and I agree. As I began to relax as I sat in a group I also began to admit to some very bad behaviour. I told the group of that time when I arrived home to find my wife ready to give birth. 'That same thing happened with my second child,' said one chap. I made a positive statement that 'I never want to become that type of person again.' I felt a sense of relief that my 'guilty secrets' were coming out into the open. I faced the stark facts that I had been 'a right selfish bastard' during my marriage. Addiction removes loyalties to others. Practising addicts think only of their next supply of the substance to which they are addicted.

Group therapy helps a person to assess their own character. I did not like what I had become as I remembered my selfish actions that had deprived my wife of housekeeping money. There is more to sobriety than merely stopping drinking. Character assessment and making necessary changes takes time and practice. Having first established that there is much work to be done and that only the supreme effort is good enough, then the alcoholic should begin to realise that such things are in the future. There is a need to aim for certain goals that will take more than just one day. Such was my thinking and my spoken word. Despite my enthusiasm and determination, I suffered from bouts of anxiety during the nights that I spent alone. I wondered what the future had in store for me. I realised that I could not spend the rest of my life living in a small attic.

I thought of the future. Where would I live after I left the bedsit? Would I meet a woman with whom I could form a permanent relationship, and what type of job would I look for? There were — and still are — many questions to be answered. Oh, yes, indeed, there is more to sobriety than merely ceasing to drink alcohol. Those people who seek help early can save their marriages and their career, and so a group is made up of people who are at various stages of recovery or addiction. All have different circumstances away from the unit. I began to realise that because of the vast differences in circumstances there had to be differences in some of the ideas that were put forward. I could not follow the advice of a married man who said, 'I took my wife dancing instead of to a pub.' Tolerance was again being learned as I sat through some meetings during which the topic under discussion did not apply to me. Suggestions on how to avoid a divorce and persuade a partner to support the patient did not apply to the already divorced, but we listened patiently.

As I lay on my bed at night I would recall many events of years gone by. Years of dereliction or years of my boyhood after WWII. Memories of a drunken father and of brutality. I recalled the almost hysterical screams of my father as he demanded to see the flow of blood. 'Blood. I want to see blood!' Sadistic urges being shouted at two sweating young lads who fought bare-knuckled for the enjoyment that their actions gave to their 'master'. I recalled the tears of frustration, and the feel of knuckles that smashed into teeth, nose, or eye. 'More action!' screamed the only person enjoying the fight. As blood flowed from swollen lips, and yet more blood ran from swollen noses, a request would be made: 'Let the poor bairns stop now, they are both bleeding.' The master answered the plea that had been made by Mother. 'Do you call that little bit of red stuff blood? I want real blood and plenty of it from the mamby-pamby pair of bastards!' And then, 'I'm going to make men of you bloody weaklings.' Mother would be told to stop interfering when she pleaded for an end to the fighting. Michael took up boxing at the Hull Boys Club and did quite well. Father had scorned him by saying such things as 'You will be out of your depth at a club.' The night that Michael proved the master wrong by winning a prize, he was given a beating by the man who hated to be proven wrong.

As I lay in my bedsit at night with just the ticking of my clock to break the silence, I would sweep away those memories of the past as I began to feel the pain of abstinence. My determination to win the fight for sobriety was never to weaken as I suffered stomach cramps, a dryness of the mouth and feelings of fear. Cold shivers ran through my chest as though icy water ran through my veins. 'Electric shocks' ran through my arms if I attempted to straighten those arms. I became fearful of death. 'I'm going to win. I'm going to win,' I repeated over and over again as the depression of vagrancy fought to stay with me. I likened myself to the fictional Dr Jekyll who fought to stop the beast from taking him over. I was to be more successful than the poor doctor. I put my theory of inner conflict to the group during a therapy session. The drinker versus the abstainer. Some said it was a good way to see our problem. It highlighted that already known fact — 'I am the problem.' I told myself that I was glad of the suffering for it showed just how much damage alcohol had inflicted upon my body, and I used that suffering as a deterrent.

As the weeks of treatment began to pass I realised that there was more to do than just speak of 'one day at a time'. I had a whole new life to construct. I had a future that was hopefully going to last more than just a day. I wanted to look further forward than that. I had no idea at that time of just how badly damaged I was and that my recovery was to take years. I thought of forming new relationships with non-alcoholics, and perhaps of finding a special person to give me the happy husband and wife relationship that had been my dream. Where would I find such a companion? Drinking clubs were not places which I intended to frequent in the future. 'Where will I live when I leave this bedsit?' I was already thinking of bettering myself. I often voiced my opinions that 'One day at a time is alright to begin with, but surely it must be dispensed with when sobriety became strong?' I was told, 'Don't get too ambitious, pal.' Sceptics said, 'You are going to fall flat on your face.' Nine years later I am still standing, still sober, and still planning well ahead.

I continued to take trips down memory lane as I sat alone at night. I remembered little Billy Berry who had been the best-known character in Hull, the best known alcoholic. I had known little Billy since I was a young man having my first year drinking. Billy was already barred from many pubs in the town. The pub which I frequented allowed Billy to have two halves of bitter before he would be asked to leave. I shall always remember Billy with a great deal of affection for he was a perfect gentleman. It did not matter that he had fallen by the wayside and ended up as a vagrant. He was more genuine than most of those people I have met in various walks of life. Way back in those days of my youth I would laugh as little Billy spat on his hands and then rubbed them together as he said, 'I will fight anyone in this pub!' No man ever took the little chap seriously, and it was when he started to issue his pugilistic challenges that a friendly landlord would ask him to leave the premises. Billy did not give any trouble as he supped up and left.

If I had been told during 1954 that I was to end up drinking wine on a bench with Billy 25 years hence, I would have scoffed at the suggestion. I often drank on the benches with Billy, and he would provide cigarettes which he had been given. Billy did not smoke but he saved cigarettes for the other vagrants. Sandwiches he had been given would be kept in his pockets or in the large canvas shopping bags that he carried. Billy would give food to other vagrants. I only ever knew of one female who lived rough, and she became his on-off. She was named Connie and another man was to vie for her affections. He was 'Frying pan Jock' and he had a bedsit to live in. Connie went to it. The sudden demise of Connie probably hastened Billy's own death. The local Hull newspaper gave him a good write-up after his death. I submitted a poem to that newspaper (I think the year was 1984) and was pleased to see it published:

Farewell little Billy, you were part of our town,
You may have lived out, but you were never down.
Some girls have blushed at your little trick,
Of lifting a skirt with your walking stick.
Harmless actions and harmless 'Choice' words,
You showed that you had an eye for the birds.

Farewell, little Billy, sleep peaceful and bonny,
Re-united with your ladyfriend Connie.

I consider it a privilege to have known Billy Berry who really had been a gentleman of the road.

I would often be asked, 'Do you ever feel like taking a drink?' and in the early stages of my therapy I would say, 'Yes, but I do not fancy the consequences of having taken one'. I did not, as a few people did, blame alcohol for my troubles. I blamed myself for having drunk the alcohol. My reply to the question varied with time, 'I do not drink because I choose not to, I still choose not to, and I would dismiss a *desire* as being mis-placed nostalgia. I choose to remember the bad times.' I am in control of myself and my actions. I am not controlled by alcohol. It is essential for addicts to choose not to drink. There are very few people (I only know of one) who can be converted to sobriety. Threats of divorce or prison will not make an addict respond to treatment.

It is most unfortunate that some people can have a disruptive influence on others and affect their faith in group therapy. A man can be sent to a treatment centre by the courts after drink or drugs have been blamed for a crime. The person who has escaped justice by being sent to a unit has no intention of stopping drinking. Those people can influence others who are still in the process of 'drying out'. Remarks such as 'clever twat' (or worse) are made when referring to people who are doing well. To a person who is already suffering some personality disorder, the thought of being branded a 'clever twat' is not a nice one. I likened the disruptive element to those people who intimidate workers with shouts of 'Scab!' Manipulators do not wish to stick out like a sore thumb and so, the more people they can turn away from success, the less conspicuous they become. I was right when I made my drunken statements about 'a wicked world'. It is a world that I have learnt to live with.

Most people are embarrassed when confronted with a crowd of strangers. When those strangers ask about one's private life then it is all the more so. Although group therapy works so well when addicts question addicts, there were (and no doubt still are) some people who take liberties by asking very impertinent questions regarding sexual relationships. All very unneccessary when a simple, 'Does your drinking affect your marriage?' would do fine. Some of the group members (usually the non-triers) seemed to fancy themselves as prosecutors. I could never understand why impertinent and offensive questions were not ruled 'Out of order'.

One man who was a disruptive element chose females from those who were still mentally confused. The unit was the source of his succour as he preyed upon confused females. Many patients were destroyed by his actions. I hated him for his activities and his attitude. In a final attempt to manipulate yet another entry into the unit as an in-patient, he got drunk yet again. He choked to death on his vomit. There were no tears shed for him as there had been for others who died — and he went unmourned.

There were some very sad cases that reflected the effects of alcohol abuse. One man imagined himself to be Oedipus Rex and jumped to his death from a window of the Infirmary. A poor woman who could not come to terms with reality drank paraquat. She suffered a lingering death for three days before the cloak of eternal darkness gently fell upon her. A young girl took a massive overdose of barbiturates, and a young man slashed his wrists. A young woman slashed her throat. Not all drinkers are enjoying themselves.

Chapter Twelve

INDEPENDENCE!

As my mind began to clear after the permanent blur of intoxication diminished, I was faced with the problem of accommodation. I could not stay in a tiny and uncomfortable attic forever. I needed accommodation with some basic facilities. I had completed approximately 18 months of my hospital treatment, and was thinking of a future. Lady Luck was still smiling favourably.

I sat in my bedsit one evening and reflected on the meetings at the unit. There was a knock at my door and it was Mother. 'Get your coat on quickly. There is a small house to let in the next lane from the one I live in.' A part of the teachings of the unit was that I should consider all my actions. I had to throw caution to the winds and hope that everything would turn out for good. I do not like being rushed at any time but I broke the rules and followed Mother to the small house where we met the landlord. It was evening, and there were no lights in the house enabling me to view the condition of the interior. I felt uneasy at the thought of leaving my bedsit without the chance to sort out my affairs and needs, but I also thought of the efforts that my mother had made towards helping me find my own accommodation away from the bedsit and the shared facilities. I said, 'I will take it,' and Mother paid the advance rent required.

I went to Brian and told him that I had found other accommodation. He did not hesitate when wishing me luck. He did not mention notice of leaving the flat as other landlords would have done and he did not insist on a month's rent, etc.

I was due for quite a shock when I viewed the house in daylight for it had been vandalised. The one consolation was that all the windows were intact and the electricity supply was still connected. With the help of my brothers I made the house look inhabited. We fitted a lock to the front door and put up curtains at the windows. Light bulbs were fitted and left to burn so that the house could be seen to be occupied. The upstairs of the house was a wreck, and there was a huge hole in the ceiling enabling the sky to be seen. There was a hole in the roof too.

My first few weeks in the house were a nightmare. I feared that vandals would enter when I was away at the unit. I could not become a hermit, though, and so continued to travel to the hospital. Each return journey home was agony. Was the house still as I had left it? I would enter and begin a thorough search to ensure that it was empty. I checked doors and windows and the upstairs before turning the key in the front door and locking myself in. I had never lived alone before that time and I did not relish the thought of doing so. Sitting in a derelict house during vagrancy and drunkenness is not the same as sitting alone in a house when one is sober. A bedsit is not being alone, for there are other people in the house. I looked upon the situation as a new challenge and adapted so successfully that I now dread company. I have become rather set in my ways during the many years that I have lived alone: I hope to meet a woman who will 'unset' my ways.

After I had noticed the state of disrepair I asked my landlord at least to have the roof repaired. I was told that it would be seen to. Almost two years after taking tenancy that roof had not been touched. My younger brother had to make some temporary repairs after a violent rainstorm. I was to suffer some more of that 'Stinking authority' that I so despised for, shortly after having taken the tenancy of the house, a bill for electricity came through my letter box. It was for fuel supplied to the previous tenant. I sent the bill back with an explanatory note. Three days after I had returned the bill I received it back again. I could hardly believe my eyes as I saw that the YEB had simply altered the name of the previous tenant and substituted my name. There was a further re-enforcement of my detestation of 'Bumbledom' as I visited the offices of the Yorkshire Electricity Board and was told that if the bill was not paid they would disconnect me. Despite my 18 months of therapy I found it very tempting to explode into a fit of temper. With great difficulty I managed to remain calm and leave the offices. I took the bill with me to the unit and asked the charge nurses to help me. The senior charge nurse contacted the YEB and was assured that the mistake would be rectified. I still received two more final demands and a visit from an official before it was conceded by the Board that I was not responsible.

Although I began to settle down to living alone in a house, I had more troubles to endure before I finally moved because of demolition and re-housing. My next-door neighbours vacated their home a few weeks before I was to leave my home. My fears of the vandals returned now that I had an empty house next door. I was not wrong in my expectations of trouble. The house next door was soaked with paraffin and set ablaze during the night. The blaze was fortunately spotted by a watchman opposite. The fire engines were called out and the blaze was contained before it could spread into my home, but I did suffer smoke coming through a gutted and destroyed upper floor of the house next door. It was now also possible for someone to walk into my house via the upstairs of next door.

I became very depressed indeed as I imagined that all that I had achieved was about to be undone. Would my home now be wrecked by vandals? Would all my possessions be stolen? Where would I live? I ignored the welfare office who should have been dealing with my re-housing and I approached a senior charge nurse. Calls were made to Hull Corporation and my re-housing was given priority. I was suffering the shakes during those few weeks that I awaited re-housing in an area that I had requested. I wished to be near to my previous Corporation home. I suffered from a bad attack of 'nerves' after the fire. I was still not capable of dealing with traumatic situations. Thank goodness I had the unit behind me and a Corporation housing office that was a caring institution. My troubles were not yet over, though, and it was once again to be authority that made me angry. I applied for the 'upheaval' grant that is payable to all tenants who are moved from clearance areas. I was allowed the cost of the removal and nothing more. I appealed and received a visit to my flat. I had applied for curtains and floor coverings and an electric cooker. My cooker was a gas appliance. I was refused what was a request for compensation and not a request for charity! I had to go through an appeal procedure after a young woman visited my home and suggested that I 'adapt or alter' things from my old home. I was later sent a 'compensation' cheque for £3 'replacement of curtains, pots and pans, carpets and cutlery'.

I listened to other re-housed people who spoke of the hundreds of pounds that they had received. I was able to apply what I had learnt during therapy. I had a decent home that did not have a leaky roof. I was not afraid of this accommodation being easily entered via a burnt-out shell next door. I also took into account that I was near to my old home and so used to being in that area. Although I had only just moved into my flat, I was already deeming it to be much better than the house that I had just left and so began to think in a positive manner. I had been sad as I took one last look around the old house. I owed a lot to that old building for it had been a stepping stone in my recovery. I had learned to live alone, and I had developed a sense of pride in my home. Scruffiness, untidiness, non-payment of rent, all those bad things that were associated with my drunkenness, were gone.

Bare floors and a lack of decor decided me that I would 'take a break and visit the bingo hall'. It was a Saturday afternoon and there was a link-up with other clubs for one big jackpot of over £300. I WON IT! I could hardly breathe as I waited for just two numbers at an early stage of the game. Both of those numbers eventually came in succession. I endured just two more days in a furnitureless flat. Yipee! I decided then that 'fortune does indeed smile upon the righteous'. That road which had seemed so long at my outset of the journey towards sobriety and a life within the community was growing ever shorter. I became more relaxed, and steeped in nostalgia. I wondered if my beloved Margaret was still living in Ulster. I wondered about those vagrants who still lived out in the cold. I recalled childhood memories. I was happy, I was relaxed and I was content. My contentment with my new surroundings enabled me to relax and remember some of my less fortunate friends. The ex-marine Bob who had died so young. I recalled how Bob had taught me how to make the intricate pieces of ceramics which I had sold for drink, and I remembered those things that Bob had made so well. Rainbow fish with small mirrors where normally painted eyes would have been, and Starfish, and land animals. Yes, Bob had been a good lad, a good friend. Bob had helped me when I was having a 'bit of a rough time' on the road. A much needed drink had come from Bob as I buckled beneath the ravages of vagrancy. Bob seemed to think that adding water to his whisky would reduce the effects that the drink would have upon his ulcer. He died of a perforated ulcer shortly after he had just obtained a job. He had a pregnant girlfriend, and he told me that he was 'happy at last'. Poor Bob. He literally 'drank himself into the grave'. All very sad.

My visits to the bingo hall became less frequent as I gained confidence in myself. They had played their part and that venue had become just another stepping stone in my journey towards a strong sobriety. I had learned how to use restraint as my feelings of being 'talked about' threatened to turn me into a recluse. I still suffer from feelings of inferiority, and feelings that people are 'talking about me' but I do not walk away from a situation as I used to, nor do I become angry and aggressive. I exercise (with great difficulty!) restraint as I tell myself that I am imagining that I am the topic of other people's conversations — conversations that are scornful of me.

Despite my 'shyness', as I prefer to call my feelings, I wanted to further myself and seek the company of unmarried women. The women who attended the bingo hall were all either married, dedicated spinsters or far too young. I had found the visits to the hall to be very beneficial and I recommended that other patients with 'crowd problems' try it. A lot of the patients did just that, and benefited from the experience both mentally and financially. There were a few happy faces during therapy meetings.

Reality was present and I suppose it was beneficial to me to learn that I could not escape gossip mongers and animosity born of envy. Winners were given some filthy looks, and much 'backbiting' went on during the intervals. Yes, I did indeed 'learn a lot about life' at the bingo. I cannot change society. I can only change myself so that I adapt to it.

Chapter Thirteen
ABSENT FRIENDS AND OTHERS

My two years in uniform provided me with some pleasant memories as I sat in solitude during the early days of abstinence. There were also many sad memories.

Shortly before my demob I had made a keepsake/memento plaque containing my shooting medal and cap badge, and shoulder flashes and hackle. I sold the plaque some time in the 1970s for the price of a bottle of wine. When I sold the plaque I thought of men with whom I had served. There were so many nights when I did not need a television or a radio, for my memories could provide me with all the entertainment that I needed.

Not all my memories were pleasant ones and I would (and still do) wonder who was responsible for the burial of those characters who died on the streets. It is difficult to imagine Hughie or George lying dead in some morgue as the authorities decided what to do with their bodies. All those men who die unwanted and unmourned are often in my thoughts, and I cannot help but feel sadness for all those poor souls who still trudge aimlessly through the streets.

No more cheery waves from little Billy Berry. No more encouragement from that little chap as he said — of my effort to achieve sobriety — 'Keep it going, kid.' I always stopped and had a chat with Billy. There were many more sad deaths, but names escape me: so many different faces passed through the unit during those years when I fought not only for my sobriety but for my sanity.

'If' was one word that played a large part in my thinking for quite some time after I had ceased drinking alcohol. If I had been told of alcohol treatment centres during my years with my wife and children, would I have taken treatment? If I had been financially secure during the 1950s, would I have remained in Ulster and married my beloved Margaret and have become a convert? If my father had listened to the advice of my school teacher would I have been able to go on to further schooling and tutoring in English? Perhaps I would have become a writer *if* I had been allowed the chance to learn. If I had not been on 'Skid Row' would I have ever learned how to appreciate the simple things in life? If I had *not* gone down skid row then I doubt that I would have ever written this book. If I had carried on drinking I would now be dead. I would have died a pauper and passed unmourned.

Such thoughts as my possibly having died in some derelict house or overgrown cemetery weed patch often crossed my mind in those early days of treatment, as would thoughts of those poor ragged individuals who shuffle along the streets cursing some unseen adversary. Men who blot out reality and memories of cruel blows which fate has bestowed upon them. If only I could help them I would. Mentally ill men who are called 'habitual offenders' by some magistrate who sends them to prison — men who should have been given the sanctuary of a psychiatric hospital.

I often came upon old men who were still suffering the after-effects of WWII. Old men who would sit muttering of 'Bastard Germans' or 'Bastard Japs'. I met some of those men in prison. I still think that I am right about society. It stinks! I see society as a small band of 'Silver spoon in the mouth' people. The rest of the people on this island are slaves to those few. I wonder how many of those judges who called a shell-shocked vagrant a 'dirty little individual' had ever fought in the war.

Men who should be inside a psychiatric hospital are languishing in gaols or sitting staring at blank walls in a so-called 'home' which has replaced the hospital. I often pass those bleak houses where people sit in chairs for most of the day as they stare into space. Perhaps some of them are remembering those days when they had large grounds to walk in and a large canteen to sit in, and a rehabilitation centre to dance in. That, of course, was taken from them with the closure of the hospitals.

It was on July 26, 1988, that I paid my final visit to Broadgates Hospital. It was a special farewell visit, for the axe had fallen on that hospital and unit just eight years and seven months after a ragged and homeless hobo begged for professional help.

Spring

How nice to see the green grass grow
From beneath the melting snow,
And birds that left the winter's cold
Start returning to the fold.

Hedgehogs awake from winter's sleep
And new-born birds begin to cheep,
Lovers in their hearts do sing.
All are signs that this is Spring.

The Vagrant

He carried his goods in a paper bag
That vagrant without a home,
That man who had no family
That man who had to roam.
He had to roam the streets each day
For nobody cared to know,
A man from a closed institution
A man with nowhere to go.
He was a drinker. He was not a thief.
He was not a murdering brute.
He was simply a victim of cirumstance —
A patient 'Given the boot'.

'Given the boot' from a hospital
Where he had received great care,
But now the hospital was closed
And the man lived in great despair.
Society shunned him. They called him a 'Nut'.
They resented him living nearby,
He'd never done harm to anyone —
Why did they fear him? Oh why?
Taunted by children and scorned by adults
He was driven from his new home,
And a gentle soul with the mind of a child
As a vagrant the streets he does roam.

Poverty

Hard was the crust of the mouldy bread
Which was served in the workhouse grim,
Hard was the hand of the Beadle
Who led young boys in hymn.
Hard was that birch which rose and fell
Inflicting pain on the lad,
Hard was the heart of the Beadle —
Broken was the heart of the lad.

Orphans and waifs feeding on gruel
Hardly the stuff for body fuel!

Skinny young lads. Pale and thin,
Bones protruding almost through skin,
Poverty stricken and fever racked
Desolate, broken, spirit cracked.
A racking cough, a cry in the night,
Death relieves a lad from his plight —
Death from poverty does not save
As a lad is lowered in a pauper's grave.

Highgate

To the Gutter and Back is a remarkable book written by a remarkable man.

Len Bromby, born in 1937, was praised at school for his ability at English, but, like most boys of that period from working-class homes, he had no opportunity of continuing his education to a higher level. School was followed by a variety of manual jobs, interrupted by National Service, and with increasing problems as he became more and more addicted to drink. He went to prison, his marriage failed, and he ended up as a down-and-out, roaming the streets of Hull by day and passing the nights in the squalor of derelict buildings.

It is a tragic story, yet not depressing — because **Len Bromby** is a gifted writer with a powerful style, and he describes his experiences with a verve which makes you eager to find out what happened next.

His vivid, colourful descriptions of everyday life in the back streets of Hull in the Forties and Fifties, a way of life now gone for ever, are surely destined to become a much-quoted source for future historians of the city, and the intense emotion re-created by his account of a family tyrannised by a sadistic father is totally convincing evidence of the seeds of later tragedy being fatally sown in childhood.

To the Gutter and Back is the odyssey of a Hull man's descent into Hell: an inspiring one, too, which ends in victory after a long and arduous battle against addiction.

In recent years many words have been written about the problem of homelessness, but nothing as revealing and memorable as **Len Bromby's** journey **To the Gutter and Back.** In **Len Bromby** these people, usually regarded as the outcasts of society, have found an articulate spokesman to tell their side of the story.

HIGHGATE is a company producing good quality, readable books at reasonable prices. Its publishing list includes titles of both general and local interest.

ISBN 0 948929 36 7 **£5.85**

Highgate Publications (Beverley) Limited

VARSITY RAGS
AND
HOAXES

F. A. REEVE

STUDENT RAGS have almost disappeared from the Cambridge scene, and even the annual events to raise money for charity cannot rival the former "Poppy Days". The present-day undergraduates have to take their studies seriously, and the many who came up merely to enjoy themselves are no longer with us.

This book recalls some of the rags and hoaxes of the past, such as the classic Shah of Persia and Sultan of Zanzibar hoaxes, the night climbers of King's College Chapel and other buildings, the men who hung a car below the Bridge of Sighs, and those others who performed the much more amazing feat of hoisting an Austin van to the roof of the Senate House.

F.A. REEVE'S previous books include *Cambridge* (Batsford 1964, o.p.), *Victorian and Edwardian Cambridge from old photographs* (Batsford, 1971, o.p.), *Victorian and Edwardian Cambridgeshire from old photographs* (Batsford, 1976), *The Cambridge That Never Was* (The Oleander Press, 1976), *Cambridge* (Batsford, 1976), *A Historical Walk Through Cambridge* (Newton and Denny, 1976), and *The Cambridge Nobody Knows* (The Oleander Press, 1977).

Front cover illustration:
Safely Home! (F. Keene) *Cambridgeshire Libraries Collection*

Back cover illustration:
One of the 22 beds on wheels which took part in a 12 mile race during the February 1977 rag *(Cambridge Evening News)*